CW01635447

How Do I Look?

How Do I Look?

Theology in the Age of the Selfie

Dominic White

scm press

Published in 2020 by SCM Press
Editorial office
3rd Floor, Invicta House,
108–114 Golden Lane,
London EC1Y 0TG, UK
www.scmpress.co.uk

SCM Press is an imprint of Hymns Ancient & Modern Ltd
(a registered charity)

Hymns Ancient & Modern® is a registered trademark of
Hymns Ancient & Modern Ltd
13A Hellesdon Park Road, Norwich,
Norfolk NR6 5DR, UK

British Library Cataloguing in Publication data
A catalogue record for this book is available
from the British Library

978 0 334 06001 7

Typeset by Regent Typesetting
Printed and bound by
CPI Group (UK) Ltd

Contents

Acknowledgements

When Agnès Varda made her first feature film, *La Pointe Courte* (1955), she announced that it was 'A film by Agnès Varda and the inhabitants of La Pointe Courte'. Writing is necessarily solitary on one level: *I* have to write my book. But many people have contributed insights and ideas: the Margaret Beaufort Institute of Theology in Cambridge, which has given me the warm and nurturing context of a Research Associateship for the writing of this book, and my good friends and colleagues there, especially Férdia Stone-Davies, Anna Abram, Amy Daughton, Louise Nelstrop, Melanie Prejean and Elizabeth Powell. Douglas Hedley and all at the Plotinus Seminar at the Cambridge Divinity Faculty were most helpful on the Platonist tradition, and Silvianne Aspray introduced me to Nicholas of Cusa. Among my Dominican confreres, I must thank Timothy Radcliffe for his encouragement and many perceptive and helpful comments on my drafts; Aidan Nichols, for his expertise on the icon and bibliographic support; Benoît Vandeputte, who welcomed me so warmly at our Tours priory and has supported this project from the French end, as well as Christian-Marie Donet for access to the Archives of the Oratory of La Sainte Face. I am also grateful to the Dominican brethren in Lund for their suggestions for reading and especially my community here in Cambridge who have supported this writing project and helped me out with my duties. Likewise, the students at the Newcastle Catholic Chaplaincy taught me much about phones, social media and the issues they pose for the gaze, as did my colleague Mia Fox; also Bryan Vernon, Alison Merritt-Smith, Lydia Hiorns, Lorna Bryan,

Rob Hawkins and all the team at Shieldfield Art Works (formerly The Holy Biscuit), LIFE Newcastle and Molly Bythell. Special thanks to Marie Pavlina Kašparova OP, Veronika Hliničanova, Anna La Mura, Zlata Vrabec, Marianna Nodale, Rupert Shortt and to Michel Jouannolle for his expertise on Lacan and Christianity. And of course my patient and encouraging editor David Shervington and his team at SCM Press. And the couple I was talking with on the 15.11 from Leeds to Bristol.

1

How Do I Look? The Crisis of the Gaze

Does being Christian change how we look at others? How they experience our gaze? How *we* feel seen, how we feel about our image? It should do – according to Genesis 1.27, humankind, therefore each and every person, is made in the image and likeness of God. In seeing the other, I see God's image. And Jesus taught that the other is my neighbour whom I am called to love (Mark 12.30–31).

But this question has become all the more urgent here and now when a major UK Government-sponsored study has revealed a crisis of social media-related body dissatisfaction among adolescents (Kelly et al. 2019). Can Christians – not just by their words, which are often unwelcome in a secular society, but by the bodily action of their *gaze* – give to others a positive experience of being seen?

How do I look, then? Of course, I am playing on two possible senses of look – the acting of looking at another and how I look *to* another. Looking is about the gaze, about seeing and being seen. It is seldom about one person seeing, alone, unseen. The look is about my appearance and one would be hard pressed to claim that there is never a note of anxiety, no desire for approval, for acceptance, for love.

Of course, it has always been there. People have always compared and judged and criticized, with words, with a gaze, or with silence.

And beauty has always been ideal and impossible. Few if any real people have looked exactly like the ancient Greek statues that still occupy dominant places in museums and with the process of ageing, time always wins. Perhaps, at least implicitly, these statues have been understood to represent a Platonic idea of beauty in which we 'particulars' can participate to a greater or lesser degree. It starts from our awareness of other people, who are different from me. I *perceive* them as being fatter/thinner, shorter/taller, fairer/darker etc. than me and, depending on the ideals of the culture(s) I inhabit, these differences may make me feel better or worse about myself. So my looking at others, my gaze, is culturally programmed to be critical (how I look *at* others) and self-critical of my own image (how I look *to* others).

But the ideal, varying across cultures and epochs, can frequently be oppressive: for example, nineteenth-century upper-class European women were commonly expected to wear corsets, tight-laced to narrow their waists, which recent medical experiments have demonstrated caused reduction to lung capacity (Steele 2001, p. 71). Today, we have a female thinness culture and male muscularity culture that many women and men simply don't fit. The gym, the swimming pool and the beach, which should be places of recreation and pleasure, can become a nightmare. Especially as there is always the fear of someone taking a furtive snap on their phone while we are changing and posting it on social media. Cruel and insulting comments can follow, in a realm which has the potential to enable such good conversations, but more often is devoid of courtesy and used as an outlet for rage.

As human beings have always compared themselves and others, the current crisis of social media-related body dissatisfaction among adolescents (and others) cannot be blamed wholly on digital manipulation or social media, and with fundamental physical changes to the body during adolescence, at least some awkwardness about self and others is perhaps inevitable. Nevertheless, the proliferation of digital media (self) images on Facebook, Instagram, Snapchat, etc. have massively raised the *impact* of the image of ideal beauty. Photographs are supposed to record what is *really* there, not just an 'artist's impression'. Yes, we know that lighting and focus can flatter: they are the photographer's equivalent of make-up. Physical airbrushing of photographs, to remove 'blemishes' and enhance features deemed attractive, existed long before Photoshop, but Photoshop is much easier to employ. Indeed, such digital manipulation can make fundamental changes to appearances in a photograph such that the images of celebrities on the covers of magazines are *not real*. They have been retouched to look like an ideal of beauty which corresponds to no real person, but looks as if it does because it is a photograph. The critical/self-critical gaze now has the measure of an impossible reality, an *un*reality. As far back as 1996, Julian Stallabrass commented that with the then rising phenomenon of digital photography, the editing of a messy world into digital perfection 'threatens to proliferate an ideological sameness ... a new wave of blandness ... the conventional beautiful' (Stallabrass 1996, p. 34; see Jurgenson 2019, p. 98).

And indeed, physical make-up has gone beyond what you see in real life. Rather, 'real life' is now the camera's view, the social media view on your phone. We want to really look like what social media and photo-altering technology permits. 'Instagram Face', part of the 'quest for hyper-perfection', which has dominated social media since 2015, is defined as 'Photo-perfect skin and sculpted, contoured cheekbones, wide almond-shaped eyes which taper up into a feline point, and that full, inescapable mouth' – inspired partly by the models Twiggy in the 1960s and Kate Moss in the 1990s (Jones 2018). As this is what gets the most likes on Instagram, therefore there's an urge to look like this in real life, which with the amount of make-up involved (and time applying it) is not sustainable – and all to try and look like someone who doesn't exist, an ideal like the Greek statue.

But while we can edit to our heart's (dis)content, the question of digital editing starts with a technical problem. The smartphone, which brings together for the first time the camera and social networks in one device, also has a physical problem: the selfie-camera on these phones can only be held as far away from my face as the arm will stretch. That is not far enough to prevent me from looking like a fish. So in most phones, unless we switch it off or use a selfie stick, a filter uses an algorithm to make our face look 'normal'.[1]

Normal: a word with so many implications. To make my face look normal, does that mean to restore the image to what the eye naturally sees? For example, to remove 'red eye'? To edit out the glare from a spotlight? Or does it mean to remove 'blemishes' and offer 'the best possible me'? If it is 'the best possible me', then just what is that? Whose idea of best?

As we've seen, the question of 'whose idea of best' has always been there in the ideal(s) of beauty. It's not just my idea, it's society's, 'theirs'. And the selfie is, as Nathan Jurgenson says, a *social* photo. It's bad enough for someone to snap me in the changing room. It's far worse that they can spread it all over social media, where I can appear before the merciless tribunal of beauty. However, things are more complex than that. We like social media because it connects us, stops us feeling lonely. As Jurgenson says, we should not 'conceptually preclude or discount' all the ways intimacy, emotions, even evil, can pass through a screen (Jurgenson 2019, p. 82). And I, personally, am much better at remembering friends' birthdays thanks to Facebook.

But, says Jurgenson, the shared selfie is both an outlet and an audience for self-documentation. We can get likes and followers. Of course, we can then get anxious if we don't get as many as we want, as we feel we 'should' (or, even worse, get none at all). Yet sharing pictures can be a pictorial way of chatting (notice how predictive texting increasingly offers images instead of words). Jurgenson argues that, unlike the traditional processed and printed photograph, which documents what is already past, a nostalgia, an indicator of mortality,[2] the social photo 'instead emphasises an ongoing exchange, a springboard to future action and dialogue ... By being quick, the temporary photograph is a tiny protest against time' (pp. 49–50).

The trouble is that another physical fact about the selfie is that it is necessarily a photo of me taking a photo of myself. It is not even like a self-portrait: rather, it shows me looking at me, *my gaze on myself*. It attaches image-taking and sharing technology to 'the traditional workings of identity', which it makes more explicit. 'Selfies make plain the ongoing process of identity construction' – which is perhaps why they are often deplored (p. 55). Perhaps a photo with friends is different (an 'ussie'? The word never seems to have caught on), though again, if I post it, it is a story of me and my relationships and tells others that I have friends, so I am successful.

But what I regard as my self is, according to Jurgenson, 'what you think others see when they see you' – what they think your inner truth is (p. 57). Christians might question this definition (we will explore this more later), but if Jurgenson is right – that this is what most people, however unconsciously, understand their self to be – then it is perhaps not surprising that the possibility of 'enhancing' my appearance in selfies, beyond removing 'red eye' or glare, is a very attractive option. And while more or less tyrannous ideals of beauty have always been with us, we see from Julian Stallabrass's analysis that I can easily construct my self according to 'an ideological sameness ... a new wave of blandness ... the conventional beautiful', and 'rate' others accordingly. And this beautiful self is disembodied: 'Because digital images can be altered and edited with the aid of computers, they are not the same sort of "witness" as analog photos that are made more literally of light bouncing off the world' (Jurgenson, p. 98).

If I can add a personal observation, during my seven years as a university chaplain I was struck by the intense social and aesthetic conformism of the large majority of students I encountered. That's not to say that rebellion and bohemian eccentricity should be compulsory (they too can be conformisms), but there seemed to be a real fear of departing from a certain unconscious but very visible norm. Yet is it really surprising in a society that might be characterized by 'surveillant anxiety' (Crawford 2014), 'camera consciousness' (McCosker 2015) and a general awareness that cameras are distributed everywhere, from phones to drones? Facial recognition technology is normal and so, sadly, is image-based bullying.

So take a phone where you can shuttle between camera, social media and the internet (infinite source of 'ideal' images) with a touch and you have enough material to trigger a mental health crisis. Even in 2004, before the universalization of smartphones, Marika Tiggemann and Brenda McGill conducted a study of 128 undergraduate women at a South Australian university, investigating the link between adverts and poor mental health (Tiggemann and McGill 2004). Existing studies indicated to them that current societal standards for beauty 'inordinately emphasize the desirability of thinness, and thinness at a level impossible for many women to achieve by health means' (p. 23) and that the gap between the average woman's body and size and the 'ideal' size was bigger than ever before (think of the employment of peripubescent models who are often naturally thinner than adults). The results of Tiggemann and McGill's study confirmed their hypothesis that when women were presented with adverts, 'the amount they actually focus on appearance and compare their overall appearance and body parts with the image predicts negative mood and body dissatisfaction' (p. 37). 'Body-isms [photographs of just parts of a body, such as a leg or a stomach] ... elicit just as much social comparison and produced as much negative affect and body dissatisfaction as full-body advertisements' (p. 39). Actually, body parts had the highest mean score for body dissatisfaction, which Tiggemann and McGill suggested could contribute to larger social effects, such as objectification. And of course Photoshop has been available since 1990, which means that the adverts in the study may have shown not just teenagers, but people who actually didn't exist.

The impact of media on body image is not confined to women. Daniel Agliata and Stacey Tantleff-Dunn (2004) examined the impact of TV advertisements on males' body image. A group of 158 males with a broad height and ethnic distribution were selected for the study. One group was exposed to advertisements with ideal male body images, the other to advertisements with neutral images. It was found that exposure to images of the ideal male (lean and muscular) can significantly increase one's dissatisfaction with one's own musculature, whereas non-appearance adverts had no such effect. Viewing ideal males also led to a significant increase in depression, but exposure to neutral advertising had the opposite effect. Agliata and Tantleff-Dunn noted that, at the time, the average person was exposed daily to nearly 25 appearance-related adverts, based on an average of 2.4 hours per day of watching TV – 150 per cent more adverts than in the experiment (p. 19). 'Television and magazines exacerbate this problem by presenting airbrushed, artificial images as real' (p. 9).

It is noteworthy that a journal entitled *Body Image* was founded in 2004, the same year as Agliata and Tantleff-Dunn and Tiggemann and McGill published their articles. And since then, with Photoshop and other applications enabling us to retouch our *own* images on social media, the whole issue has risen to a new level. Jennifer S. Mills, Sarah Musto, Lindsay Williams and Marika Tiggemann carried out an experiment on the 'effects of selfie taking on body image and mood in women' (Mills et al. 2018, p. 87). Previous research that Mills and her colleagues drew on found that women aged 16–25 spend up to 5 hours per week taking and uploading selfies on their personal profiles on social media sites such as Facebook, Instagram and Snapchat, which suggests that this activity constitutes a significant part of young women's lives. Mills and her colleagues investigated an ethnically diverse group of 113 female psychology students at York University, Toronto. They were divided into three groups: those who could upload a photo and not retouch it, those who could upload a photo but were allowed to retouch it, and a control sub-group who read an article from social media on an unrelated topic (travel) and then answered questions on it. It was found that, post-experiment, anxiety went up the most with the untouched selfie sub-group and still went up significantly with the retouched selfie group, but actually dropped a little in the control group (perhaps because of relief that the questions were over!). Confidence dropped in all cases. Feelings of physical attractiveness decreased by similar amounts for both untouched and retouched (slightly more for retouched) but actually increased a little for Control. Perhaps we feel more attractive when we feel clever? There were 'null effects on stated feelings of fatness, satisfaction with one's body, and depression' (p. 90), but Mills and her colleagues noted that a selfie shows only the face, not the whole body (clothed or unclothed). (This suggests an area for future research.) Being allowed to retouch multiple times did improve self-image compared with untouched, but that sub-group were actually less confident than those posting no selfies at all. Mills and her colleagues suggest by way of explanation that

> it could be that scrutinizing and modifying images of themselves makes women think more about their flaws or imperfections. Retouching could activate feelings of self-objectification. Even though self-presentation strategies like photo-editing provide a sense of control over physical appearance [...] they do not actually appear to improve mood or self-image. (pp. 90–1)

Of course this does not make social media bad in itself: Mills and her colleagues acknowledge how it can aid well-being through a greater sense of interconnectedness. But clearly technology that enables one to retouch one's own image to an unreal and perhaps impossible state of beauty is increasing the already harmful effect of the ambient thinness culture on young women's mental health.

Another way this thinness culture is manifested is in 'fat talk' (sometimes called 'body talk'). Rachel H. Salk and Renee Engeln-Maddox (Salk and Engeln-Maddox 2011) researched this phenomenon, which they define as '[i]n general ... characterized by women (typically peers) engaging in mutual disparagement about the size and shape of their bodies' (p. 18). Among 168 undergraduate students at a private university in the US Mid-West, 84 per cent of the participants were in the normal weight range. The study found that 93 per cent engaged in 'fat talk' regularly with friends and believed that others did it more than them. For the experiment they were asked to write a script to continue a conversation that began 'Ugh, I feel so fat'. The top score was denial ('No, you're not fat!'). Approaches also included sharing a strategy such as dieting or going to the gym. Probing ('Why do you feel that way?') came much lower. Much of the motivation for 'fat talk' seemed to be seeking reassurance, and the most common view among participants was that words of reassurance brought relief, though some believed it made it worse ('If you're fat, then what am I?'). Some participants also expressed annoyance at the pervasiveness of body image concerns among women and admitted feeling manipulated to affirm a friend's body image. Salk and Engeln-Maddox acknowledged that sometimes 'I'm so fat' is an idiom for distress, a call for help, group solidarity, and even a pre-apology for eating a lot. But what is significant is that the idiom is based on the thinness culture. They admit that the participants were largely mono-ethnic and some research suggests this is less of an issue among non-European American women (Spanish, Mexican, Black).

The international General Data Protection Regulation (GDPR) of 2018, although not aimed at the self-image crisis as such, may have some benefit. It seeks to protect individuals' privacy regarding data, which includes photographs of them (Information Commissioner's Office 2018). Of course, face-recognition technology enables people to carry out image searches on search engines, not just tagging photos of Facebook friends. GDPR may protect people to some extent (for example, the change from 'opt out' to 'opt in' with regard to the use of photographs of or including people), but there is a vast amount of data held through website cookies and in search engines, and to whom are they accountable? We seek more privacy, even as we seek to see and be seen. And as Tiggemann and McGill point out, the big issue is the predisposition of individuals to comparison, and they propose that future research should focus on persuading women and girls not to compare themselves with others (Tiggemann and McGill 2004, p. 40). It is hard to argue with this, but it would require a drastic change not just to our culture, but to global human behaviour. And it has become intensified in modern, Western urban culture precisely because the body is at the centre of personal and social life. As Regina Ammicht-Quinn says, 'churches and museums have been superseded by fitness studios' (Ammicht-Quinn 2009, p. 72). But she also points out that this has brought new problems: the body culture has engendered a body cult. Bodies can be successful or unsuccessful, they can be enhanced. A weak male body or a fat female body become causes for shame. 'Saying no' is no longer about sex, but about food (pp. 72–4).

As a Christian, I would say that any proposal to shift away from body appearance comparison is so fundamental that it needs not just action but the miracle of divine grace. But what can Christianity offer to this question of the image and the comparative gaze? Can my gaze transform the other person's self-esteem and self-perception? And what needs to have happened in me – in terms of my self-image and my image of the other?

In Chapter 2, to understand what we mean by the gaze and the issues surrounding it, I will look at the philosophies and psychologies of the gaze of Jean-Paul Sartre, Jacques Lacan, Laura Mulvey and Michel Foucault and at Emmanuel Levinas's views on the face.

In Chapter 3, working from my experience that much of the actual philosophizing in our society is done by artists, I will examine some works of art that offer alternative gazes: Agnès Varda's film *Faces Places*, Molly Bythell's painting *where is the laptop*, the *WE ARE WOMEN* photography project, and the image of Christ's face at Tours that is believed to be miraculously produced.

In Chapter 4, I look at vision and the divine gaze: ideas about vision in contemporary society, and the desire to see/contemplate/be seen and transformed in Platonist philosophy that has so shaped Western imagination and thought. In dialogue with this cultural and philosophical setting, I examine the idea of seeing (or not seeing) God's face in the Jewish Scriptures/Old Testament, its fulfilment in Jesus' gaze in the New Testament, and his teaching on how we should look.

In Chapter 5, I look at the gaze in the early Church, as witnessed by the New Testament and early Christian rites of baptism.

In Chapter 6, I will look at the gazes of the Church in the icon, the eucharistic presence and seeing our brother or sister, concluding with an examination of Nicholas of Cusa's *Vision of God*, which brings together the gaze of/on God and the gaze on the other person.

In Chapter 7, I examine the thorny question of the erotic gaze and the chaste gaze. Can a gaze be both erotic and chaste? Does celibacy have a particular redemptive gift for the gaze in an age of hypersexualization?

In Chapter 8 I re-read the psychologies, philosophies and art of the gaze in the light of what we have discovered about the Christian gaze as potentially transformative and divinizing in a digitalized and increasingly tribalized age, when embodied action that opens a conversation may be the most powerful preaching of the Word.

Notes

1 I am indebted to Pavlina Marie Kašparova for this information.

2 He is drawing on Susan Sontag's *On Photography*, which we will discuss in more detail in Chapter 3.

2

Seeing and (Not) Being Seen: Philosophies and Psychologies of the Gaze

Them versus me?

In the last chapter we looked at the crisis of self-image in our society, noting especially the role played by the selfie shared on social media. A complex, conflicted relationship emerges between self and others, self and society. On the one hand, we are social beings. Social media connects me up with others and I can share pictures of myself and enjoy their likes and comments – hopefully. But 'hopefully' is the problem. What if they don't like me? What if I don't get any comments? Or instead receive negative, cruel and insulting comments (including offline and behind my back)? To maximize my chances of likes and positive comments, I can 'enhance' my image. What makes my image enhanced? Conformity to standards of beauty which 'they' impose – standards that come to me through media, especially the internet, which is as accessible on my phone as my camera and social media apps.

The social and the personal are at the heart of the question of the gaze, so philosophers have approached the gaze in two ways – from the standpoint of society looking in on the individual, and from the standpoint of the individual looking out on other individuals and on the world. The two perspectives are of course inter-related – society conditions the individual's gaze and perceptions, but also society is made up of individuals. But given the social impact of the selfie, we begin with Foucault on two kinds of social gaze, before going on to Sartre and Lacan on the gaze(s) of the individual.

The Clinical Gaze and the Gaze of Surveillance: Michel Foucault

For Michel Foucault, the gaze is constructed socio-politically. In *The Birth of the Clinic* he argues that, partly triggered by the French Revolution of 1789, fundamental shifts occurred in medicine in the eighteenth and early nineteenth centuries that in turn changed the gaze. The doctor emerges as the expert on illness, having a gaze that is pure, naive in the best sense, 'enlightened', describing simply what he/she sees (unlike the pre-Revolutionary doctor who was a member of an elite guild with their privileged knowledge). This naive gaze quickly became a problem when people fell victim to charlatans, so the next project was state-educated and state-organized doctors. The pure gaze was now also the expert gaze that 'sees' the disease in terms of interpreting the symptoms both visible on the surface and invisible inside the body, which can be determined by questioning the patient or carrying out tests (Foucault 1973, pp. 38–65).

But this does mean that the doctor no longer sees *this person*, but instead classifies 'the patient' in terms of their disease. Prior to this medical revolution, the locus of medical care was the family, and the focus was on loving this person, giving them gentle, spontaneous care, to assist 'nature in its struggle against the illness, and allow the illness itself to attain its own truth' (p. 17). The gaze was one of love. Of course, in practice the care may have been more or less loving, and in itself could offer little or no successful medical treatment. But it saw *this person*. The organization of hospitals and the problem of funding care for the poor, as well as paying for the education of doctors, meant that the clinic and medical school were combined. As a mark of gratitude, the poor were expected to offer themselves as subjects. Foucault says, 'But to look in order to know, to show in order to teach, is not this a tacit form of violence, all the more abusive for its silence, upon a sick body that demands to be comforted, not displayed? Can pain be a spectacle?' (p. 84). And the emphasis on dissection of cadavers also leads, Foucault argues, to a focus on the patient as *dying* person – the illness that can kill them.

Foucault is not denying the massive benefits of modern clinical medicine. But clearly something has been lost in the shift of the ideal of care from relationship (home, the family) to the clinic, where the person becomes a body of spectacle: a gaze that inspects the disease rather than loves the person, a touch that probes rather than comforts.

Foucault was writing in the 1960s. Since then, there has been a remarkable rise in complementary medicine, which can be attributed to a great extent not to its proven clinical effectiveness but to the *personal* attention of the therapist. The therapist's gaze that seems to see the *whole person*, the listening (which deals with the emotional side of illness), the touch that is experienced as *healing* (see Furnham 1996, especially pp. 73, 77). Simon Singh and Edzard Ernst, who have carried out extensive and deeply critical research on complementary medicine, admit that the 'gentle touch and calming manner' of a craniosacral therapist can bring a relaxation response (Singh and Ernst 2008, p. 282). Whereas a cold, stern doctor of the 'old school' who sees not me – my exposed body – but a disease, makes me feel anxiety and shame. His or her gaze certainly doesn't help me feel better.

Shifts are taking place: witness the British National Health Service's Shared Decision Making approach, which

> brings together the individual's expertise about themselves and what is important to them together with the clinician's knowledge about the benefits and risks of the options. This means that lay expertise is given the same value as clinical expertise. (NHS England 2018)

So a recognition of many patients' desire to be more involved in their health care, of a certain *equality of gaze* between doctor and patient as they work together on the illness. If the patient wants craniosacral therapy, though, there is no guarantee they will get it: patients are not permitted to choose treatment options that are not supported by clinical testing. And some patients are reluctant to engage with the programme. The 'Expert Patient Programme' was in fact applied in the first instance to patients with chronic illness, the main argument being its cost-effectiveness (Rogers 2001; Shaw 2004).

Turning to the wider impact of the medical gaze, how often do we see the gaze of people in general as inspecting and classifying us (whether or not this is their real intent)? 'Thinness' can so easily be seen as 'not overweight'... And so Photoshop 'cures' in an image the 'imperfections' of a body found by the inspecting gaze – an image that only reinforces the perception that I am sick with a lack of (socially defined) beauty ...

In *Discipline and Punish*, Foucault traces a historical transformation in the punishment of criminals and the state's imposition of norms of behaviour. The translator, Alan Sheridan, notes that translating the title was problematic: the French *surveiller* 'has no adequate English equivalent'; 'supervise' has different connotations, 'observe' was rather too neutral, even though Foucault was aware of the aggression involved in one-sided observation. Foucault himself suggested *Discipline and Punish*, 'which relates closely to the book's structure' (Foucault 1977, Translator's Note). But primarily *surveiller* means 'watch over', which is far too benevolent in English, though the loan word 'surveillance' comes close. The point here is that this is a *gaze that controls*.

So Foucault traces a shift in gaze as follows: in France before the mid-eighteenth century, the king's body was the object of a gaze in grand public ceremonies – the sight of the king was intended to awe his subjects. The criminal's body belonged to the king and was subject to often very public punishments, including execution. A different gaze started to emerge with the French Revolution of 1789: punishment of the criminal should be more humane, reformatory rather than punitive. For the body, this has meant being 'caught up in a system of constraints and privations, obligations and prohibitions'

(Foucault 1977, p. 11): not just crimes and offences are judged and punished, but also anomalies, infirmities, maladjustments, effects of environment or heredity, drives and desires in the individual (p. 18).

Thus the state now observes the populace. This had already started in the seventeenth century with the quarantine systems that attempted to contain the plague. Then in the eighteenth century there were the great military reviews; next, boarding schools, poor houses, hospitals and, especially, prisons. In all these, every aspect of behaviour, from dress to gesture and, especially, a person's location, could be minutely regulated (monastic rules and architecture were one source of inspiration). A culture of discipline and efficiency had been born (Foucault 1977, pp. 139–94). The keeping of records also meant that those in charge knew a great deal about each person – whereas before, Foucault's argument suggests, the individual was relatively anonymous, with only his or her actions being punished if they infringed the law. Jeremy Bentham's panopticon ('all visible') design for institutions, especially but not only prisons, was perhaps the ultimate expression of this spirit of surveillance and the automatic functioning of power. The tower in the middle and the ring on the outside brought about '[a] real subjection ... born from a fictitious relationship' (p. 202). The inmates know that at any moment they can be seen, even if in fact at that particular moment no one actually sees them.

Superficially, this is a long way from Western society today. Dress, self-expression and lifestyle have been liberalized immensely in the past 50 years (and it may not be without significance that Foucault was a sexually active gay man at a time when this was treated as an illness and a crime (Eribon 1991, pp. 26–9)). Nevertheless, schools, hospitals and prisons are normative, prescriptive and disciplinary. The state possesses a large amount of information about all of us. And the profiling carried out by search engines through algorithms, and even potentially through the camera on our computers, means that information is being stored about our private interests, desires and correspondence, information that is accessed by marketing tools (not to mention identity thieves). And of course CCTV cameras. And our profile on social media (who might be looking at my Facebook page as I write this?).

As per the panopticon prison, it is not that we believe we are being watched *all* the time: it is that we know that we may be watched at *any* time. Subconsciously, we are aware that we are under a panoptic gaze. And we alter our behaviour accordingly.

Seeing you seeing (me): Sartre and Lacan

Now we turn to the individual gaze. The presence of another person, according to Jean-Paul Sartre, changes my world. He imagines that he is alone in the park. Then he sees another man, who has his back to him. In this,

> [w]e are dealing with a revelation which is without *parts*, given at one stroke, inside of which there unfolds a spatiality which is not *my* spatiality; for instead of a grouping *towards me* of the objects, there is now an orientation which *flees from me*. (Sartre 1956, p. 254)

Because the man looks at the scene in *his* way, effectively my gaze is no longer sovereign. The effects are mitigated if the man is reading and not looking at what I am seeing. And that is without the man seeing me (although of course there is that potential). The psychoanalyst Jacques Lacan comments that this is the gaze that surprises me. It is not a seen gaze (the man has his back to me), but a gaze that *I imagine* in the field of the Other: in other words, how I imagine they are looking in their field of vision (Lacan 1978, p. 84).[1]

Immediately we see the power of the gaze of the other: even an imagined gaze has a great effect. Linguistically, it is crucial to understand that 'gaze' translates the French *regard*, which can have the senses both of looking and judging (like 'regard' in English). All the more, then, Sartre's example raises the question of how we feel about another's gaze. True, the sovereignty of my gaze is lost by the entry of another person, one who can also potentially see me. But what if the other's presence, and the otherness of their gaze and the otherness of what they see, are a potential gift to me? Perhaps there is gain as well as loss? In his critique of Sartre, Emmanuel Mounier[2] argues that we should move away from a self-centred approach towards one of 'availability' to a positive influence and regard from the other. I am not self-sufficient, so I have something to gain, not just to lose. I am no longer stuck, but my destiny opens to new possibilities. Mounier was writing in the 1940s, long before the omnipresent screen of the mobile phone that absorbs all my attention, but his words are strangely prophetic:

> [The other person] robs me, in effect, but he robs me of myself as enemy of myself, from my self-centred opaqueness, from this burden and *screen* that I am for myself in my solitude. (Mounier 1947, p. 138, my translation and emphasis)

Whereas

> everyday experience tells us the revelatory value of the advice of others when given with good will, or simply the clarity (*lucidité*) which they awake in us by the simple, silent weight of their gaze. But left to our own devices, our self-knowledge and self-assessment is poor. (Mounier, p. 138)

Mounier argues that even a hostile gaze can be of value if we are 'available'. (Maybe 'open' is a better translation.) Not, of course, available/open to harm, but rather to what may be of truth – he gives the example of atheist critiques of religion (at a time when Christian apologetics could be very defensive and not open to the listening they demanded of others).

But can this be applied to the gaze? My atheist colleague, even if he/she does it rudely, may expose an inconsistency or superficiality or hypocrisy in my beliefs and arguments and the way I express them and this is clearly of benefit to me even if stinging at the time. But to cast a negative, hostile judgement on another person's appearance is not to rebuke their action but to attack their very *being* – to attack who they are, how they look, what they cannot change and have no reason to change. Even a gaze, a comment on my action (dancing badly in a Facebook photograph) may be an existential attack on me ('Loser!') rather than a critique of my action.

We will return to this question in a later chapter. First, let's look more at Lacan. As a psychoanalyst, Lacan's primary concern is with the individual and his/her relations with others. The first key stage is when as a child I recognize that the person in the mirror is me. Thereby I know that this is me and not another person. And I acquire an image of myself. But I also know that I can be seen, and thus be 'other' to someone else. I am tipped into 'the drama of primordial jealousy' that, for Lacan, will mark my relationship with social situations. We desire the other, yet are in competition with them, and indeed just asserting ourselves is a risk. It 'makes the *I* into that system for which every instinctual thrust constitutes a danger, even though it should correspond to a natural maturation' (Lacan 1968, p. 75). This is because I know the other may not like, or may feel threatened by, what I am doing (or, in the case of the selfie, how I look). But also, when something (maybe quite inanimate, like a tin can) provokes my gaze, something of me, the subject, seems to slide away – according to Lacan, because this thing changes my world. Hence for Lacan, in that respect, even inanimate objects 'see' me, because of the change they impose on 'my' world.

Drawing on Maurice Merleau-Ponty's *The Visible and the Invisible*, Lacan argues that the gaze of the other(s) is pre-existent: 'I see only from one point, but in my existence I am looked at from all sides,' in the spectacle of the world (Lacan 1978, p. 72). And, of course, I see others seeing, and they can see me seeing them. When I realize that someone can see me looking (at them or at someone else) I feel shame (Lacan 1988, p. 218).

But if I see the eye of a person looking (or who I imagine to be looking) at me, their gaze disappears. Does that mean that my seeing the other seeing me neutralizes the effect of their seeing? Perhaps. And it may have other effects, according to Lacan: he speaks of the satisfaction 'of a woman who knows that she is being looked at, on condition that one does not show her that one knows that she knows' (Lacan 1978, p. 75). But is she satisfied? Does she necessarily want to be looked at? If she does, does she want to be looked at *in the way someone is looking at her*? Lacan does not consider this. The problem is the heavily Freudian basis of his philosophy of the gaze: 'The gaze is presented to us only in the form of a strange contingency, a symbolic of what we find on the horizon, as the thrust of our experience, namely, the lack that constitutes castration anxiety' (pp. 72–3). For all the obscurity of this passage, it is fairly clear that for Lacan everything is reducible to sexuality, and only that. So the gaze must necessarily be not just an erotic gaze, but the kind of erotic gaze which wants only to possess the other sexually for one's own gratification without any loving pre-intention for one's desires. The Lacanian gaze treats the gaze of the other only as competing with my gaze. It may be that we both want the same thing *for ourselves*, but we do not want each other *as other and existent in that other's own right*. We are left pessimistic about the gaze.

But as Martin Jay says, 'Permanently "downcast eyes" are no solution to these and other dangers in visual experience' (Jay 1993, p. 592). There are other possible gazes: for Timothy Radcliffe, a pre-existent intention to love, a loving disposition, means that the first stage in loving someone, including erotically, is rejoicing that that person exists.[3]

Nevertheless, Sartre and Lacan have uncovered some truths. Christians wanting to offer a different, more loving gaze in the age of the selfie cannot close their eyes to truths about fallen human nature, our shadow side, or we will rush in with good intentions and fall at the first hurdle. We human beings *are* self-centred. We do like our private worlds, and we often resent the presence of other people (how many advertising photographs of apparently unspoilt, 'secret', 'undiscovered' landscapes and beaches are devoid of people?). How often do we tell ourselves fictions about the reality of our attraction to others? How often do we feel shame when we see someone looking at them or at someone else? How often do we tell ourselves that someone else 'needs' us to be their friend, that we are 'helping' them, but actually it's our own unconscious needs that we are seeking to meet? We are gazing on them, but refusing the truth of their gaze.

So for all the limitations of their thought, perhaps Sartre and Lacan hold up a useful mirror for us. Lacan himself allows for the possibility of a different gaze on the part of God, in the case of icons, such as Christ in glory (Pantocrator). He says that icons hold us under their gaze, but that the real motive of icon-painting is that the God the icon represents is also looking at it, and the icon is intended to please him (Lacan 1978, p. 113). Or is it? We will return to the icon in Chapter 5.

Cinema and the male gaze: Laura Mulvey

The challenge of Lacan's analysis of the gaze prompted film scholar and film maker Laura Mulvey to use Lacanian/post-Freudian psychoanalysis as a political weapon in cinema. In her seminal article 'Visual Pleasure and Narrative Cinema' (Mulvey 1975), Mulvey argues that woman is the object of the gaze, whether of the invisible camera and the audience (whose gaze is thus denied), or of the characters within the film. For Mulvey, woman is the lynch pin, but 'it is her lack that produces the phallus as a symbolic presence' (p. 833).

This analysis is itself phallocentric (what about women viewers in the cinema?). But it is hard to deny that 'the magic' of classical Hollywood film is 'its skilled and satisfying manipulation of visual pleasure. Unchallenged, mainstream film coded the erotic into the language of the dominant patriarchal order' (p. 835). The alienated subject gets a glimpse of satisfaction through 'its formal beauty and its play on his own formative obsessions' (p. 835). The mass of mainstream film and its conscious conventions portrays a 'hermetically sealed world which unwinds magically, indifferent to the presence of the audience, producing for them a sense of separation and playing on their voyeuristic phantasy (sic)' (pp. 835–6). This is enhanced by the darkness in the auditorium that separates the spectators from one another. We project our ego fantasies and repressed desires on to the protagonists – as in, one might argue, Lacan's example of the child looking in the mirror. And, of course, we have an ideal projected on to us, whether of the active male or the submissive female.

Following Bud Boetticher, Mulvey argues that in classic Hollywood films the woman is important only for the love or fear she inspires in the male hero, but counts for nothing herself: she is just an image, in every sense. Even more 'artistic' films, such as Jean-Luc Godard's *Méprise* or Alfred Hitchcock's *Psycho*, often display a male-erotic, and indeed sadistic, gaze on women, a gaze which may, as Mulvey describes it, expose complicity in the viewer. But at the end of Hitchcock's *Saboteur*, the man, who in many ways has been domineering, is at the top of the tower with the woman who has become his equal partner in defeating their enemy: the couple gaze at each other against the backdrop of the sky. There is a sense of the woman completing the man, indeed their completing each other. As a believing if intermittently practising Catholic, Hitchcock would not have been unaware of Genesis 1.27: 'In the image of God he created them, male and female he created them.' Does Mulvey's rather dogmatically Lacanian/post-Freudian approach, which necessarily passes everything through a sexual and phallocentric lens, perhaps miss out on other gazes that appear in classic films, gazes of which the film maker him/herself may even be unconscious?

Nevertheless, it is hard to disagree with Mulvey that many important issues get left out of the classic Hollywood model of narrative cinema: she gives such examples as the relationship of the female infant to the symbolic word and the sexually mature woman as non-mother. Most of the time, though, it is a man who is behind the camera.

And Mulvey's analysis can also be applied to much visual art: while we might consider it a mark of maturity and broad-minded education that we can distinguish between 'lad mags' and classical female nudes, the latter are not so innocent. It does not take long to realize that many of them, as the works of male sculptors in complex socio-political-economic structures, are products of an eroticized male gaze that is as idealizing and commodifying as the classical Hollywood film and Photoshop. Further, this gaze is also often colonial: as Fikret Yegül says, the popular, fanciful paintings of female nudes in Turkish baths by the celebrity Victorian painter Sir Lawrence Alma-Tadema reflect 'a privileged, Western male view of the beautiful naked world of Turkish women' (Yegül 2010, p. 226). In other words, pornography for the educated Western male.

However, 20 years after 'Visual Pleasure and Narrative Cinema', Mulvey and Roberta Sassatelli considered that the use of Photoshop and other digital means of image manipulation in cinema makes films closer to animations. The body just becomes a manipulable object, whereas in pre-digital film 'the body speaks of itself in ways that other objects can't' (Sassatelli); the 'something more', the 'uncertainty of the human' doesn't enter in (Mulvey). Mulvey acknowledges that, unlike animation, what one might call ordinary cinema effects a 'ghostly preservation of the (once upon a time) animate human body' (Sassatelli 2011, pp. 138–9). Notwithstanding the arguably phallocentric gaze, what one sees is at least an image of a real body, a real human being. There was, according to Mulvey,

> always something that could slip, evade ultimate directorial or, indeed, human control. As Bazin puts it, 'outside the hand of man' ... Although always subject of, in Dziga Vertov's term, 'the mechanical eye' or, in Walter Benjamin's, 'the optical unconscious'. (Mulvey 1975, p. 139)

So, ironically, digital manipulation has disclosed other gazes from the pre-digital era.

The Face of the Other: Emmanuel Levinas

I had not intended to discuss Emmanuel Levinas, because he very seldom mentions the gaze. But one of his major themes is the face. In November 2018, I visited a confrère at the Oratory of the Holy Face in Tours, France, where there is a nineteenth-century print of the 'Veronica' (Figure 3.4[4]). The 'Veronica' (the name Veronica derives from the Latin-Greek 'vera icon', 'true image') is a cloth which, according to tradition, Jesus caused to be imprinted with his face when a devout woman wiped it for him as he carried his cross to Calvary. Miraculous healings are attributed to the oil which is kept in front of the copy of the 'Veronica' in Tours. And on the image, Jesus' eyes are closed. *He has no gaze*. It is we who gaze. On Jesus' face there are marks of tears and blood. One cannot look at this image and not be moved.[5] And it moved me to read a philosopher who is concerned with the face.

For all the temptations to reduce the face to the physical face, for Levinas the face does not correspond to the physical face as such. In *Totality and Infinity* he names the face as '[t] he way in which the Other presents himself, exceeding *the idea of the Other in me*' (Levinas 1969, p. 50). The face precedes all our attempts at philosophy and ontology (what things are). Levinas draws on the work of Franz Rosenzweig, who opposes an Idealist conception of philosophy as an autonomous system that grasps the All (totalization). Rather, when this system is destroyed, we are opened up, and we reconstitute the fragments *relationally* – God and humanity, which means God for humanity, subject for object, self for other (Rosenzweig 2005, especially pp. 33–4, pp. 252–6). God reveals, to individual persons. This is the basis of Levinas's contrast of totality and infinity: totality is a whole in which all apparent contradictions are resolved, to give a complete system, whereas infinity reveals the whole as inhabited by what it cannot contain. An exposition cannot be made of this – we can only be *exposed* to it (Levinas 1969, especially pp. 35–40 and 194–7).[6] We certainly cannot start with a preconceived system (however unconsciously), but rather have to see the face of the Other.

Indeed, the face of the Other may shatter my preconceptions. So ethics precedes ontology, in the responsibility that the face of the Other imposes on me: 'The face of a neighbour signifies for me an unexceptionable responsibility, preceding every free consent, every pact, every contract' (Levinas 1981, p. 88). Levinas does not regard the face of the Other in primarily malevolent terms, as a gaze seeing my gaze that examines or controls (Foucault), or of having a gaze of desire and/or fantasy that denies the subject (Lacan/Mulvey). Rather, the gaze of the Other is a moral imperative to which I must respond:

> 'He is looking at me' – everything in him looks at me; nothing is indifferent to me. Nothing is more imperative than this abandon in the emptiness of space, this trace of infinity which *passes* without being able to enter. (Levinas 1981, p. 93)

And that gaze is of a face that accuses me – maybe even if his/her eyes are shut and he/she doesn't literally see me. His/her face is 'given over to my responsibility, but to which I am wanting and faulty. It is as though I were responsible for his mortality, and guilty for surviving' (p. 91).

As Susan Handelman says, one cannot but see here Levinas's experience as a Holocaust survivor (Handelman 1990, p. 75). The Nazi regime, before recognizing him as this person Emmanuel Levinas, defined him as 'a Jew' (ontology before ethics): a form of definition that rejects the other, assimilating a person to some people's idea, to what Levinas calls *the Same*. But Levinas survived where six million others did not. And even beyond this, Levinas seems to identify with his persecutor, insisting that we recognize that other *as other*, and not as assimilated to my Same. One might ask whether Levinas, as an ex-prisoner of war, was suffering from Stockholm Syndrome. But does this question not risk putting ontology before ethics (look how dangerous our knowledge of being can be ...), and thus not seeing a deeper ethical truth in Levinas's 'Saying'? 'Saying' is the good 'rhetoric' of the dialogue of faces which he opposes to the so-easily excluding 'Said' of propositions. Commenting on Levinas's identification with his persecutors, Handelman says, 'One can see why this becomes an almost "unsayable" position. It also has strong Christian echoes and moves beyond Jewish tradition' (Handelman, p. 76).

Behind Levinas's philosophy of the face is the Hebrew word *panim*, 'presence', literally 'faces' (Levinas was not only a philosopher but also a scholar of the Talmud, the great corpus of Jewish oral law). *Panim* is the Jewish Scriptures' word for the presence of God: God being present is an encounter of faces. Related to *panim* is *panah*, 'turn': I turn to the face of the other when he/she calls me. As Franz Rosenzweig says, it is when God calls my name and I say 'Here am I' like Abraham (and not like Adam, who hides from God) that I am drawn out of isolation and experience revelation (Rosenzweig 2005, pp. 163–70; Handelman 1990, pp. 72–4). And when that happens, I am opened to love of God and neighbour. This turn towards the face radically changes my perspective.

Though, as Handelman says, Levinas inverts Rosenzweig's path: 'the immediate and pressing face of the other awakens the ego, and traces the otherness of a divinity otherwise than being, otherwise than any theology, escaping of any logos' (Handelman 1990, p. 74). Because there is a danger that if I love my neighbour because I see the image and likeness of God in him/her – that is, I do this because it is my religious duty – then I will simply project on to my neighbour my predetermined image of God (a Said). *So I will not see that person and therefore not see the trace in him/her of God who is otherwise than being.*

However, Levinas holds on to the concept of revelation while rejecting the idea of unveiling (even though the Latin root *revelation* literally means 'unveiling'). According to Colin Davis, 'The truth it [the word] contains is not *dévoilement*, the unveiling of something present from time immemorial; in Levinas's account it is a revelation, an unforeseen and unforeseeable breach within what is known and knowable' (Davis 1996, p. 47). This also gives us a key to the difficulty of Levinas's language, the appropriate difficulty of describing the task of working towards a good gaze, towards what I will argue in later chapters is a theotic gaze. Much of Levinas's writing is very opaque, and critics tend to respond by smoothing out the kinks (Davis 1996, p. 135). But the face of the other is both familiar (a human being present to me) and strange (it is *this* unique person). Hence the difficulty of Levinas's task:

> The rhetoric of presentation, demonstration, description and truth implies the existence of a stable, knowable reality which the philosopher can explicate; hence, such rhetoric relies upon the ontological assumptions which Levinas wishes to elude. In order to say the other-than-Being, language must be torn away from such ontological assumptions. (Davis, p. 135)

At the same time Levinas is aware of the potential disaster for his work to succeed as philosophy if it shakes off propositional structure.

But for all the difficulty of Levinas's prose, it is hard not to be moved by it. It is a saying that emerges from behind a veil of language. Levinas does not do the philosophy for us: rather, he somehow calls us to a responsibility to *do* philosophy by allowing the face of the other to impress itself on our consciousness, even if that shatters us. Admittedly, there is the question of what happens if the gaze of the other is malign, threatening: but maybe the task for Christians is still to see that other as more than his or her gaze, as one acting from a wound, a wound carried in the blood and tears of the ungazing face of Christ.

Perhaps even more radically, Levinas rejects light as a metaphor for knowledge – light that is a universal of religion, spirituality and art as well as a philosophical metaphor: 'Light makes objects into a world, that is, makes them belong to us' (Levinas 1978, p. 75/48). This is reminiscent of the Enlightenment light of the clinical gaze in Foucault: an unvarying, totalizing light which enables the specialist, however well-meaning, to look and analyse on his/her own terms. Certainly, without light we can see nothing: but perhaps first we need to acknowledge our own darkness, our own unknowing of the other?

We need help in order to see. And in fact that help is all around us: philosophy of the gaze is being done all the time by artists, who, conscious of malign gazes and their effects, resist by imaging different gazes in their work. So they do not just show us pictures of people, but show us how those people look – and how the artist is looking at them. They offer a different 'light'. And just as Levinas calls us to see the face of the other, so we, the viewers, begin to philosophize on the gaze in response to what we see. So in Chapter 3 we shall look at four works of art: a film, a painting, a photography exhibition, and the mysterious image of Christ from the Oratory of the Holy Face.

Notes

1 See also Lacan 1988, p. 215.

2 I am indebted to Pierre-André Mauduit OP for referring me to Mounier's critique.

3 Private emails, 14 and 17 November 2018.

4 All images are available to view online at: https://scmpress.hymnsam.co.uk/media/74923/images-for-how-do-i-look.pdf.

5 We will discuss this image in more detail in Chapter 3.

6 For a useful summary, see Davis 1996, pp. 55–6.

3

Different Gazes: Four Works of Art

A film

At the same time as writing her seminal article about the male gaze in the cinema, Laura Mulvey was visualizing a different gaze in her film *Riddles of the Sphinx* (1977), made with Peter Wollen and now considered an avant-garde classic. It tells the story of Louise, a housewife and mother in a failing marriage, obsessively caring for her daughter yet feeling confined. Once her husband leaves her she has to take a job, as a telephone switchboard operator, and negotiate childcare. Through her friendship with Maxine, a British black African woman whom she meets at the kindergarten, she becomes involved in a campaign for better childcare for workers, then finally moves to live with Maxine. But this film is much more than a story: Kimberly Lamm describes it as an 'essay film' (Lamm 2018, p. 234), which includes a short introductory lecture by Mulvey and other non-narrative sections. As E. Ann Kaplan points out, Mulvey and Wollen 'are committed to the avant-garde film, believing that we need new cinematic and linguistic forms if people are to move beyond old ways of seeing old ideologies, particularly as these affect women' (Kaplan 1979, p. 135).

The film is intellectually rigorous (there are lengthy quotations of Lacan), and, containing as it does a film within a film, it is reminiscent of the (self-) conscious cinema of the French New Wave (Bresson, Godard, Marker, Truffaud, Varda, etc.). But as Kaplan says, the ability to respond positively to the film 'seems to depend on the degree of familiarity with, and/or appreciation of, some of the new theoretical developments in film as reflected in the screen of the 1970s' (p. 135). It has moments of great beauty, such as the dream conversation between Louise and Maxine, or the use of the 360-degree rotating camera, which reverses direction as Louise and Maxine start to 'return' to a posited matriarchal model of society. But if we don't know at least some of the theory in advance, we will miss the significance of the gaze, and indeed we risk not being able to *see* the film properly at all. In reality, although Mulvey and Wollen broke the mould and opened the possibility of new gazes, their film is fully accessible only to intellectuals.

So Kaplan thinks that it would be better to use familiar forms in new ways to challenge old concepts (p. 143). And that has begun to happen: to cite just two examples, there is, first, Nadine Labaki's *Caramel* (2007), about three women, two Catholic, one Muslim, who run a beauty parlour in Beirut. They are revealed as major actors and forces for good in the challenges and conflicts faced by their neighbourhood, which are shown to be very different from, and traversing, the political/sectarian divisions. Another landmark is *Cagney and Lacey*, a 1980s TV series about two New York women police detectives (Gamman 1988). Both take quite traditional forms (romantic comedy, detective thriller) but challenge assumptions and gazes.

But perhaps the most brilliant film maker in this field is Agnès Varda (1928–2019), herself part of the New Wave movement. I was chatting about my research with a member of our congregation in Cambridge and she promptly recommended Varda's *Faces Places* (*Visages Villages*, 2017), which combines a deep exploration of the gaze and the symbolic with a very approachable and heart-warming story.

Like the other New Wave film makers, Varda's work is marked by abstraction, a non-linear structure, subversion of convention, playfulness and/or self-consciousness, and often has film itself as a major subject. But there is a unique aspect that sets Varda apart: her receptivity towards the people she films. In her first feature, *La Pointe Courte* (1955), she had already refused the implicit solitary controlling gaze of the film maker, by stating a plurality of authorship: 'A film by Agnès

Varda and the inhabitants of La Pointe Courte'. In this simple gesture she broke down the opposition between camera and subject (or, to put it better, subject and object). *Daguerréotypes* (1975) was a tender and whimsical documentary about her neighbours in the Rue Daguerre in Paris and their relationships. (Varda was short of funds, so restricted herself to the range of the longest power cable she could find that would connect to her home electricity supply.) *The Gleaners and I* (2000) is similar in character, playing on the meanings of the word 'glean' – harvesting crops or anything else from the edges, and learning bits of information. In *Faces Places* (*Visages Villages*) (2017), her penultimate film, she continues her fascination with people and their stories – also addressing the complex issue of the (self-) image and social media.

After an introduction in playful animation, setting the tone, Agnès teams up with 33-year-old photographer and muralist 'JR'. How did they meet? Not on the road, not at a bus stop (Agnès couldn't wait three minutes), nor even at the baker's (the two last éclairs JR asks for have already been taken by ... Agnès) and certainly not on the dance floor. No, they got in contact because he admired her films and she admired his mural photographs. So they are already seeing the other in their art, delighting in them and seeking to know them. JR has a van that is a travelling photo booth – people go inside to be photographed, then a few seconds later an enormous print emerges from the picture of the camera lens on the side of the van. On the camera lens rim is inscribed 'The Inside Out Project', which has a significance to which we will return.

So far, of course, it's had to be staged, as indicated with the three references to how they *didn't* meet. But then they decide to hit the road together, driving to often-forgotten corners of France. Now it is documentary and, as Varda comments to JR, chance has been her best assistant. The film maker voluntarily relinquishes control.

In a depressed former mining town in the north, the last resident of a row of condemned houses, Jeanine, is holding out. She tells the story of growing up in a mining family. They photograph her in her window, and cover her house with the print (which of course the younger people of the village snap on their smartphones). Jeanine's photo becomes a symbol of resistance, and also a meditation on decline – Agnès comments on her own physical decline, and her desire to fill holes in her memory with meeting new people. In the sunny south, a faded photograph of someone's great-grandparents becomes an enduring symbol of love. People take selfies in front of it and post them on social media. Something inter-generational is happening. Thus beautiful young Nathalie is photographed in her friend's dress – she in turn becomes a mural, which goes viral on social media. But Nathalie is not so happy about her celebrity status: 'I'm pretty shy,' she says. The problems of the image and social media come into play, and are left unresolved.

Agnès is delighted to discover that the local factory workers like to go to the cinema. But they don't all know one another, because they work different shifts – so a group photograph with faces, hands and gestures brings them together. Then, with typical Vardan whimsy, Agnès and JR put photos of fish on the side of a water tower – 'because fish live in water' (though Agnès can't get more than halfway up the steps). Then we see that they took the photos in the fishmongers – focusing on the eyes. Then it's a minor operation in an eye hospital – a connection to a horror scene in Luis Buñuel and Salvador Dalí's surrealist film *Un Chien Andalou* (*An Andalusian Dog*, 1929). Then we find out that the eye in the operation belongs to Agnès' – one of the regular injections she needs for her deteriorating eyesight. A photo of the opticians with eye test letters is done in a way that moves the letters up and down, reproducing her blurred vision of the world. Agnès compares this with the view through JR's sunglasses that he never takes off.

In an abandoned holiday resort project in Normandy they put on a festival, reinhabiting the place for the day – again, people have their photos taken, and groups form around a shared table. A postman in another village talks about his role bringing supplies to older residents, and his picture on the wall celebrates him as a local hero (the postman is also a painter). In an open-air art exhibition, Pony, a local semi-homeless artist who lives 'with the universe as my neighbour' also finds his portrait on display.

Agnès admits that after each trip, she fears it will be her last – yet each time her curiosity is undimmed. One trip covers two goat farms, one where they remove the horns, the other where they don't: Agnès lets each farmer tell his story, without trying to reconcile them – though it's clear where her and JR's sympathies lie.

Then they have an argument over his sunglasses: Agnès is irritated that he won't take them off. It seems she's irritated both that he doesn't see things as they are (when, unlike her, he can see properly) and that she can't see his eyes. Long ago she'd persuaded Jean-Luc Godard to take off his omnipresent sunglasses for the vignette she'd done with him in *Cléo from 5 to 7* (1962). JR in turn is irritated by Agnès's focus on his glasses.

But they have another trip, this time down memory lane, again in Normandy, where Agnès had filmed the late photographer Guy Bourdin (1928–91). She gets JR to put her photograph of him on a house under construction (past/future), and then to pose like Bourdin by a beach hut. This latter image is put on a World War Two Nazi gun emplacement that had become insecure on the cliff top and was pushed down to the beach. Its angle is exactly right – Agnès' assistant, chance, again.

They overcome the glasses issue when JR asks her why she dyes her hair – and she meets his centenarian grandmother, who assures her he's always been like that. Next, they pay tribute to a scene in a Godard film where three people race in wheelchairs – Agnès and JR do the same in the Louvre, to see how quickly they can get across the vast gallery.

In Le Havre docks, Agnès proposes a different approach: don't photograph JR's docker friends, photograph their wives. Agnès asks them about their work and strikes, and once she has heard their stories, the photos are taken. They are put on containers, assembled by the dockers, and the container corresponding to each woman's heart opens, revealing the woman herself. The power of cinema to reveal ... Then JR photographs Agnès' eyes, hands and feet ('you're the director of my feet', she says, as she wiggles them), and puts them on the side of freight wagons, so that they can visit places she can't. Life, and yet a sign of death.

The final trip has Agnès arrange a meeting with her old friend Jean-Luc Godard at his home in Switzerland. Agnès is clearly nervous, and warns JR that Godard is unpredictable. They arrive, only to find that Godard's house is locked and shuttered. He does not answer the door, but has written a note on the porch window: the same note as he wrote when Agnès' husband died. Agnès is visibly angry and upset, though she still leaves Godard an affectionate though rebuking note and a bag of his favourite brioches. JR comforts her and is clearly troubled by Godard's behaviour. The emotions are too real for this to have been staged. We are left wondering – was this Godard's desire to pull off a *coup de théâtre* by disrupting Agnès' own narrative? The self-conscious master of uncomfortable gazes avoids seeing Agnès and thus avoids being seen by her and by us. But he comes out of it the worse: Agnès, with her interest in and empathy for others, who delights in letting them speak, in putting their 'inside out', in the words on the side of JR's van, comes across as the one who sees, and sees with the compassionate gaze, regardless of her failing eyesight. Of course, she had ultimate control: like most films the film has been edited. And the question of shy Nathalie becoming a social media celebrity against her will shows the impact of social media on the most innocent and benign cinematic gazes. But overall the impact of the film indicates an editing that *aims at seeing the other*, receptively, for who they are. In this respect Agnès Varda represents the purest achievement of French cinema in its classic form, as *une école du regard*, 'a school for seeing/gazing'.

And she is rewarded. She takes JR to sit by the lake near Godard's home and, finally, JR takes off his glasses for her. 'I don't see well, but I see *you*,' she says. The camera blurs, representing both what Agnès sees and, respecting the muralist's desire for anonymity, *allowing him not to be seen*. Learning the lesson from Nathalie? Then Agnès says, 'Let's look at the lake.' They look out, seeing the same thing – beyond the face-to-face, to the third. And the camera is behind them, so that we see what they see, and can see it for ourselves.

A painting

Next we consider a painting by a contemporary artist, Molly Bythell (b. 1995). Entitled *where is the laptop* (sic), it shows us two figures, a nude woman on the right and an indeterminate semi-nude on the left (see Figure 3.1[1]). Both are in very soft focus, and are in fact composed of shapes in different colours, against a background that partly covers the head of the left-hand figure. The title invites us to search: just where *is* the laptop? We explore the shapes, the soft colours, maybe inspired by the effect of reflections on bodies and other surfaces. Is that black shape under the right-hand figure's chin the laptop? Or is this an item of clothing she is putting on? Is the laptop hidden under what seems to be a cover under which the left-hand figure is searching? (Is that a sofa, a cloth – our gaze wanders from the figures.) Is the laptop there at all, in fact? Maybe there is *no* laptop, no screen on which images can be found for consumption and projection, where, in spite of increasing equality between women and men in society, the consuming and controlling male gaze still dominates, catching its object in the play of seeing you seeing me seeing you seeing me ... (Lacan).

The right-hand figure looks down at the possible item of clothing, not out at the painter or the viewer. She is living her life, not responding to the painter's/viewer's gaze. Perhaps she can do this because the painter is letting her be? She can be with her thoughts, just as exploring the different shapes and colours in the painting (and perhaps forgetting about the laptop) permits us to explore our thoughts, to enter into reverie. Bythell describes her paintings simply as 'a tribute to women'.[2] The key to this is that Bythell does not offer us another image, let alone the conceal/reveal game of visual eroticism. Instead she shows us *her gaze*. In *where is the laptop* we are offered a school of seeing that delights in the figure as subject rather than object, that delights in the subject's pleasure and freedom, seeing that person's life and rejoicing in it. Perhaps it offers to the viewer this possibility of being without limits – the gift of infinity?

A photograph

WE ARE WOMEN (2017) is a photography collaboration between The Holy Biscuit (now Shieldfield Art Works) and the Agape Student Life Society at Northumbria University (see Figures 3.2 and 3.3), intended as an artistic response to the problem of 'body talk' (see Chapter 1).[3] It presents photographs of women against a dark background. The subjects are clothed, but with inscriptions that the women had written mainly on exposed areas of their own or each other's bodies: for example, 'JOURNEY TOGETHER' (Figure 3.2) on the soles of one woman's feet; 'Yesterday's mistakes don't define tomorrow's path' on another woman's back (Figure 3.3). Perhaps the most moving photo is of the arm of a woman struggling with self-harm, on which is written, 'By his stripes we are healed' (Isaiah 53.5).

In 'JOURNEY TOGETHER' the light on the women's faces is striking against the black background (a completely black background, not the chiaroscuro of classical Western paintings). The women look out at us, smiling, confident. There is much more to this than just lighting positions and shutter speeds. It both implies and necessitates a certain quality of relationship between subjects and photographer. The women's gazes are not gazes of shame, nor gazes of the erotic object, nor gazes of a transactional relationship that may not even be a just transaction. However, Helen Lerski's 'warts-and-all' portraits in her *Everyday Faces* series were transactional: they were procured from an employment exchange (Sontag 1978, p. 104). Instead we have the confident gaze of people who have built a relationship with their photographer, people who are being *seen* in a positive sense, because the photographer has been open to receive them as themselves. The photographer has allowed him/herself to behold the face of the other ... In

Levinas's terms, the Saids of the inscriptions reflect not just the Sayings between the women in the photographs: they are also made sayable and *visible* by the Saying that has taken place between subjects and photographer. After all, the fact that no two people take exactly the same photograph means that what we see, primarily, is not the subject but the photographer's gaze. As Susan Sontag says, 'photographs are evidence not only of what's there but of what an individual sees, not just a record but an evaluation of the world' (Sontag 1978, p. 88). All the more when photographs include an element that eludes even the control of the photographer but is literally an exposure of the subject: 'Astute observers noticed that there was something naked about the truth a photograph conveyed, even when its maker did not mean to pry' (Sontag, p. 87; cf. Jurgenson 2019, p. 91).

This makes *WE ARE WOMEN* all the more remarkable. The 'We' of the title refers to the subjects, unlike Helen Lerski's *Everyday Faces*, which is not what the subjects called it, and was indeed a preconceived idea into which the subjects were fitted.

One might compare *WE ARE WOMEN* with the photography of Diane Arbus, who worked carefully to build a relationship with her subjects. Many of them were people on the margins of society and its norms, physical or behavioural 'freaks'. She sought to portray them as themselves, with the full-on view almost confronting the viewer. But this was *her* decision. Even though she worked not just to obtain her subjects' consent but also to get to know them and obtain their trust, in the end that was for them to be comfortable with *her* preconceived gaze (see Sontag 1978, pp. 35–41). And now, with the possibility of instant dissemination of photographs (and then the comments ...) on social media, it's not surprising that the street photographer is seen more as a nuisance than as the romantic recorder of the life observed. 'The violation of privacy [...] *is* the art itself. Resistance to the street-photographer gaze becomes another element for it' (Jurgenson 2019, pp. 93–4).

But in *WE ARE WOMEN* the subjects have worked with the photographer to help us see them as they see themselves –

somewhat as in phototherapy. There are not even captions (I have named the photographs from their inscriptions), which photographers can use to make the photograph 'speak' the interpretation they seek (see Sontag 1978, pp. 108–10). It would be an exaggeration to say that we see the women *as they are*, and equally an exaggeration to say that their own gaze and their Saying with the photographer prevent any malign gaze on the part of the viewer. Their images are still exposed. But *the subjects themselves* were not exposed to a malign gaze, but rather to a gaze that emerged from the dialogue of faces. And the power of this gaze is that it overcomes what Sontag sees as the tendency of photography to point to mortality (pp. 15–16, 70–1 and *passim*). The photograph captures a moment, but that moment has gone and the subject has grown older, if not died. The gaze in *WE ARE WOMEN* does something different: not just taking us back to a past moment, but freezing that moment for us. In Chaim Potok's novel *The Gift of Asher Lev*, the Rebbe (head rabbi) recalls to the painter Asher Lev the words of his own father. Commenting on 'God saw everything that he had made, and indeed, it was very good' (Gen. 1.31), the Rebbe's father had said that

> the seeing of God is not like the seeing of man. Man sees only *between* the blinks of his eyes. He does not know what the world is like *during* the blinks. He sees the world in pieces, in fragments. But the Master of the Universe sees the world whole, unbroken. *That* world is good. Our seeing is broken, Asher Lev. Can we make it like the seeing of God? Is that possible? (Potok 1990, p. 100)[4]

Later, when Asher goes home, his wife Devorah tells him that she is writing a children's story, 'about a little girl who discovers a cave where there is a lasting now' (p. 102).

Photography offers us back the moment lost in a blink, by freezing the moment for us. In the photograph it is eternally that moment, eternally *now*. The gaze in *WE ARE WOMEN* allows us to enter that now, beholding not just the subjects, but their gaze. We have as long as we like to learn to see as they see, how they would desire to be seen. In the freezing of time, a glimpse of eternity, a glimpse of the heavenly gaze.

The Face of Jesus? The image of the Holy Face of Tours

In Chapter 2 I mentioned my encounter with the image of the Holy Face of Tours, a copy of what is believed to be the Veronica, a cloth on which, according to tradition, Jesus' face was imprinted on the way to Calvary (Figure 3.4). Miraculous healings are reported through the medium of the oil kept before the image. Especially noteworthy, since Jesus' eyes are closed, is that reports of healings have included someone with an eye disease (Archives Tours, 2019). The encounter with this ungazing face prompted me to investigate the writings of Emmanuel Levinas on the face, but here I want to look more closely at the Holy Face of Tours itself.

There is a third-century tradition that King Abgar of Edessa exchanged letters with Jesus (Eusebius, *Ecclesiastical History* I.13). In the *Doctrine of Addai*, dating from *c.* 400, we read that Jesus sent Abgar a response to his letter, promising that after his Ascension a disciple would visit King Abgar and heal his illness, with an added promise of the conversion of all who were with him and a blessing for his city: 'may it be blessed and may no enemy ever again rule over it' (*Doctrine of Addai*, 13). Hanan, King Abgar's archivist, then painted a portrait of Jesus (*not*, note, a miraculous image). Later, during the Persian invasion, the image miraculously reproduced itself on a tile (see Ryidina 2001). The first record of the belief that the image of Edessa was not made by human hands is from the sixth-century writer Evagrius Scholasticus, who speaks of the Edessans' use of it against a Persian invasion (*Ecclesiastical History* IV.27). In the hugely popular *Golden Legend* of Jacobus of Voragine (thirteenth century), the painter is overcome by the glory of beholding Christ, and is unable to paint him, so Christ prints the image miraculously (Jacobus of Voragine, 159, p. 646) – from which comes the popular legend.

In Eastern Christianity this image came to be called *acheiropoietos* – 'not made with hands' – and is the origin of the icon of the same name (Figure 3.5). The image is also known as the *mandylion*, which literally means a small towel or handkerchief, and the name originates in a somewhat confused legend about the towel used by Jesus to wash his disciples' feet at the Last Supper, but came to be associated with a cloth on which his image was believed to be imprinted. Hence in practice it means the 'icon of the Lord on the cloth' (Cameron 1983, p. 87; Ouspensky and Lossky 1982, pp. 69, 72).

Another tradition has it that the Roman Emperor Tiberius was healed by a cloth, similarly imprinted by Jesus with his face, which a disciple called Berenice brought to the emperor. 'Berenice' transformed into 'Veronica' in Latin, and Veronica became the name given to the woman who wiped Jesus' face during his Passion (as recorded in the apocryphal *Death of Pilate*; and see Meagher 1967). This tradition has taken root, and is now one of the Stations of the Cross, the traditional Roman Catholic devotion to Christ's Passion. The name 'Veronica' also became analysed as *vera icon*, 'true icon' – that is, the true image of Christ. In her loving response to Jesus, whether she recognized him as the Lord or just felt sorry for a condemned man, in a fundamental action of charity she herself becomes the true image of Jesus, something that is possible for Christians now if they ask for grace to respond with charity to those who are suffering.

In the West, the 'Veronica' was recorded as being venerated in the basilica of Saints Peter and Paul in 1193. Dante himself records its veneration during the Jubilee Year of 1300 (*Paradiso* 33:103–111, *Vita Nova*, 40; Vettori 2003, pp. 43–51) and apparently crowds poured in year after year (Pfeiffer 2000). The images of the Holy Face of Genoa (Figure 3.6) and San Silvestro in the Vatican (Figure 3.7) are also associated with this image. The relic inspired art: by Jan van Eyck (Figure 3.8) and Hans Memling (Figure 3.9). But in 1527 disaster struck: Rome was sacked by the mutinous troops of the Holy Roman Emperor Charles V (Vettori 2003, pp. 43–51). For a long time, the relic was believed lost, but Heinrich Pfeiffer has argued that the image in the Basilica of the Holy Face in Manoppello (Figure 3.10) is the original (Pfeiffer 2000), though this has been strongly critiqued by Roberto Falcinelli (Falcinelli 2010). And there is also the question of whether the face is the same as that on the Shroud of Turin (see Pfeiffer 1986, p. 38).

Whatever the case, what is striking is that these early images show Jesus' face without wounds. The question naturally arises, could this be the image, or a copy of an image, that was made during Jesus' earthly life? A new image was commissioned in Rome to replace the lost one, based on the face from the Shroud of Turin, the Mandylion, and people's memories of the old one. But the crucial difference was that it showed the suffering Lord. In spite of very tight restrictions on copies, popular piety won out, and it was thus that the Venerable Léo Dupont, 'the Holy Man of Tours' (1797–1876), acquired his copy, set it up in his house, and miracles began (Archives Tours 2019).

Ultimately it is very difficult, if not impossible, to prove an ultimate origin with Christ himself. Certainly there are some strange features: the Manoppello image does not seem to have been applied to the cloth with paint or any other known material. But is this any more than a pious legend that has developed, as so often, by a process of Chinese whispers? As we have seen, the Mandylion cannot be traced back beyond the sixth century, though this has not stopped it accruing enormous spiritual, theological and political significance (see Cameron 1983). And it is a source of enormous consolation to the suffering, the poor, the marginalized and the desperate, such as I saw coming to the oratory in Tours, for whom the historical veracity of an image of their Saviour is hardly among their most pressing problems. Especially when the image is recorded as working miracles ... Of course such stories also attract seekers of the paranormal, commonly associated with pseudo-history and pseudo-science, which further increases the heat of the debate, but generates little light.

What can we say of it, then? According to Ouspensky and Lossky (1982, p. 69), the *acheiropoietos* icon 'receives its true meaning in the scriptural context': 'We heard him say, "I will destroy this temple that is made with hands, and in three days I will make another, not made with hands"' (Mark 14.58). So 'the image "made without hands" is above all the incarnate Word, which "shewed" Itself in "the temple of his body" (John 2.21)' (Ouspensky and Lossky 1982, p. 69). This was key in the defence of icons against the iconoclasts – ultimately all images of Christ, whatever their physical accuracy, point to the Word of God revealing himself in the flesh. We will discuss this in detail in Chapter 6.

But again, the Chinese whispers must have started somewhere, and may point to a real origin in 'the cloth which had been on Jesus' head, not lying with the linen wrappings but rolled up in a place by itself' which Peter saw when he came to Jesus' tomb with 'the other disciple' (John 20.6). One can hardly imagine that such a precious relic would be treated with indifference by the first Christians, and making copies would be a natural insurance policy.

Copies of copies are an opportunity for artistic licence. But when I sat contemplating the copy of the Holy Face at Tours, in the midst of researching the gaze, a gaze which in our society is so often experienced as judging, controlling or lustful, what struck me is the simple fact that the eyes of the suffering Jesus are closed. *He has no gaze.* He refuses the gaze. We can look how we like at him, even with anger and contempt – but he does not look back. Just as he dies on the Cross, one can say that *his gaze also dies.* And our gaze is convicted by his non-gaze, just as his innocent suffering on the Cross convicted the world of its sin. Yet all this was so that we could be redeemed, and with us our gaze.

St Thérèse of Lisieux (Thérèse Martin, 1873–97), a Doctor of the Catholic Church, had a special devotion to the Holy Face, and her official name as a Carmelite nun was Teresa of the Child Jesus and the Holy Face. During her childhood her family already had contact with the shrine of the Holy Face in Léon Dupont's house in Tours and they were enrolled in the Confraternity of the Holy Face of Jesus (Uitvlugt 1998; Gaucher 1987, p. 99).

Although, according to one of her Carmelite sisters, she saw

Jesus' face as 'the mirror in which she saw her Beloved's soul and heart ... the meditation book from which she learned the science of love' (O'Mahony 1975, p. 127), she was particularly drawn to his downcast eyes, as veiled (note Memling's representation of Christ's face on Veronica's veil). He is hidden, which she celebrates in her poem 'Living on Love' (Uitvlugt 1998). Part of the 'hiding' can be seen as a way of describing the enclosed, hidden life of a Carmelite contemplative community, devoted to prayer – but might it also be a response to the judging gaze, the seeing that does *not* see the others, but draws conclusions from a projection? Thérèse was herself one of the first saints of the camera (Figure 3.11). Though warm and friendly, she was also very private and modest, according to her sisters (O'Mahony 1975, pp. 59, 99, 149–50, 211, 248), so may not have enjoyed the experience of being photographed.

And Thérèse, for all the youthful exuberance and sweetness of her writing style, was a spiritual teacher of extraordinary honesty, an honesty born of the grace needed to endure hard spiritual trials, such as her feeling that God had hidden from her, and illness (she died of tuberculosis at only 24 years of age). And she was deeply rooted in a meditative engagement with the Bible. She spoke of herself as thriving 'under the shadow of the Cross, watered by our Lord's tears and his precious blood, with his adorable Face *for its sun*, that Face overcast with sorrow' (Thérèse of Lisieux, *Autobiography*, p. 187, my emphasis). One of her sisters wrote in her notebook that when Thérèse was dying, her community brought one of her images of the Holy Face into the infirmary for her to gaze on. Thérèse said, 'How well Our Lord did to lower His eyes when He gave us His portrait! Since the eyes are the mirror of the soul, if we had seen His soul, we would have died from joy' (Agnès de Jésus, *Yellow Notebook* 7 August 1897, 5.8.7, translated in Uitvlugt 1998).

Thérèse's words are perhaps all the more striking when they are the fruit of years of meditation before an image at once haunting and, as it were, 'hiding' from all attempts to establish concrete facts about its ultimate origins. But, above all, Thérèse's understanding is profoundly biblical: she echoes

Israel's search for the shining face of the Lord, and the dying and rising that come from the transformative impact of God's unveiled, unmediated gaze. In the next chapter we will consider the idea of vision, and what the Bible has to say about the vision of God's face and the gaze of Jesus.

Notes

1 All images are available to view online at: https://scmpress.hymnsam.co.uk/media/74923/images-for-how-do-i-look.pdf.

2 https://mollybythell.com/About. I am grateful to Molly Bythell for permission to reproduce this image.

3 I am grateful to Miriam Westfall and the subjects of *WE ARE WOMEN* for permission to reproduce these photographs.

4 I am indebted to Zoltán Körösvölgyi for bring this passage to my attention.

4

The Face of God and the Gaze of Jesus

In all cultures, even our own secular culture, there are visionaries: people who see beyond the everyday. Their vision may be of what is hidden in something, its potential – such as the potential of a brownfield site to become a wildflower garden for the local community. They may see the potential in a person – such as the child psychologist who sees in the fidgety child not just attention deficit disorder, but a dancer. There are the artists who see the extraordinary depth of ordinary things[1] in nature, people, objects and situations, and can reveal this (whether that depth is light or dark or both). We often say that such people are inspired, even if we aren't sure what they are inspired by or by whom. The spiritual visionaries are usually more explicit about the ultimate source of their inspiration. They may have actual visions of angels or saints or of God, but more often they are aware of the presence of the invisible in the depths and heights of the visible, whether that is some depth or height of being, angels, saints, or God himself.[2]

The vision changes the visionary, and changes their relationships. They are often marked by a deep, mysterious and passionate love which spills over on to their neighbours and environment. The desire to do good to the environment and the local community with a wildflower garden; to set a child free to realize their potential; to show to others something they have seen so that the others can see it too; to share the divine love that they have experienced. And in the reverse direction, as it were, falling in love can be creative, making the person (or persons) and making them fruitful.

Of course, the community activist, the maverick paediatrician, the artist, the mystic and the lover can also fall into idol worship that often becomes oppressive and abusive. To rule the community, to force another person to be the realization of my dreams, to be revered as a guru, to be loved, and yet not to love the other but only the image I project on to them ...

We read such stories of both real vision and destructive idolatry every day in the media. The issues and questions they raise are the stuff of novels, poetry and films. They are also addressed in philosophy and in the Judaeo-Christian tradition.

In the philosophical tradition of Plato and the Platonists, which started in Greece in the fifth century BC and has been foundational to the Western imagination, what is desired is to see and contemplate the Good. Vision, at its highest imaginable level. In the celebrated simile of the Cave in Plato's *Republic*, prisoners are chained up in an underground cave. They are entertained by a puppet show, lit by a fire. For want of any other experience, they presume this is reality. But what if a prisoner was set free, and dragged out and up to see the sun? They would probably resist, but once they became accustomed to the light, they would not just see, but would *contemplate* (*theasaito*) the things in the heavens (*Republic* 516A).

Something is lost in translation here: *theasaito* is the 'middle' voice of the verb, which has a reciprocal, passive and reflexive sense. They would see and be seen by the things in heaven, see in a mutual, shared gaze, being seen and seeing themselves. This meaning is obviously cumbersome as translation and interrupts the flow: but all these senses are included and their significance should not be underestimated. According to Catherine Pickstock, in the ancient Indo-European origins of the middle voice, 'There is some evidence to suggest that its use was not simply to cast an action as either reciprocal or reflexive, but to express the mediation of divine by human action' (Pickstock 1998, p. 35). So again, the liberated prisoner turns towards the stars and the light of moon until they look full on at the sun, to 'contemplate what kind of thing it is' (or 'such as it is', *theasasthai hoios estin*, *Republic* 516B). Thus to see what the sun is, as it is, to see what I am, as I am, to gaze mutually (in bedazzlement?), to see myself for what I am, as I am (for the first time?). Of course, Plato knew as well as we do that we cannot look straight at the sun without risk to our eyesight. Yet we desire the sun on our face, we wish we *could* see the sun. Even with the risk. Is this a desire for destruction that brings life?

Ascent through desire, through love, is made explicit in Plato's *Symposium*, in a speech by Diotima the prophetess and philosopher, as reported by Socrates. She charts an ascent through the lover's physical desire for an individual body, to bodies in general, then love for souls (the origin of our 'Platonic love'), then to the fruitfulness of love in activity and laws arising from the desire for the betterment of others. This opens out into a sea of beauty, to which it wants to give birth. Then, says Diotima, the lover sees 'a certain single kind of knowledge, which has for its object a beauty of a sort I shall describe to you' (*Symposium* 210d5/p. 97). Suddenly the lover will catch sight of a wondrous beauty. The Greek for 'will catch sight of' is *katopsetai*, again a middle form which in the present tense is an ordinary active. But in the future, it seems to tell us, seeing will be reciprocal, transforming – a 'mediation of divine by human action', in Catherine Pickstock's words. This beauty is unchanging, it is everywhere and nowhere, and the lover 'contemplates' (middle, of course) 'that beauty ... and is able to be with it' (212a2/pp. 98–9). Being with: relationship. The vision is fruitful in bringing to birth true virtue.

This ascent to beauty through love, often called the 'intuition of beauty', has been vigorously asserted and just as vigorously denied down the centuries, but has never ceased to haunt us. And Plato of course also speaks of the higher realm of Forms or Ideas, of the Good, the highest form, of Being and the One. Plotinus, the Neo-Platonist philosopher of the third century AD, spoke of the ascent to the One: 'we long to see, if it is in any way possible, what is the One – as it really is and not as per anything else' (*Enneads* V.5.7–9, my translation). Again, the verb 'to see' is in the 'middle' voice – a reciprocal, reflexive seeing and being seen.

The face of God: seeing and being seen

It is not so surprising that Jews, Christians and Gnostics were keen to dialogue with Plotinus: the Jewish people already knew that to be human meant to be made in God's image and likeness (Gen. 1.26–27). The Psalmist longed to see God (Ps. 42.2), and dreaded that God should hide his face (Pss 27.9; 30.7; 102.2). Moses, Aaron, Nadab, Abihu and the 70 elders 'saw the God of Israel' on the mountain (Ex. 24.10).

But more than this, Israel longed not just to see God, but to be seen *by* God: 'May God be gracious to us and bless us; and make his face to shine upon us' (Ps. 67.1; cf. Pss 31.16; 42.2). Depending on the vowels used, Moses and his companions either 'saw God' ('*qal*' = active form) or 'appeared before/ were seen by' God (*Niph'al*, similar to the Greek middle).[3] The famous blessing in Numbers 6.24–26 says, 'The Lord bless you and keep you; the LORD make his face to *shine* upon you, and be gracious to you; the LORD lift up his countenance upon you, and give you peace' (my emphasis).

And what we translate in the Bible as 'presence' is 'faces' in Hebrew (*panim*). Presence is face-to-face: so in the Tent of Meeting, 'Thus the LORD used to speak to Moses *face to face*, as one speaks to a friend' (Ex. 33.11).

Seeing and hearing – or just hearing?

As we saw in our discussion of Levinas in Chapter 2, related to *panim* is the verb *panah*, 'to turn'. I turn towards someone else to look at them, and also of course when I hear them speak (unless I do not want to be seen or do not want to hear them). Levinas shows us how the face and saying go together. But this is also a source of tension in the Judaeo-Christian tradition, starting right in the Scriptures themselves. In Exodus 33.14 God says, 'My presence will go with you [literally, 'my face'], and I will give you rest.' Moses then asks God to show him his glory. God agrees to 'make all my goodness pass before you' (a parallel with 'The Good' in Plato?) and to be gracious and merciful, 'but ... you cannot see my face; for no one shall see me and live' (Ex. 33.20). So God says that he will hide Moses in the rock and cover him with his hand, and Moses will see God's back, but not his face.

The absence of God's face is a major theme in Deuteronomy. Whereas in Exodus the emphasis is on Moses, Aaron, Nadab, Abihu and the 70 elders seeing God, in Deuteronomy Moses tells the people that they heard a voice speak out of the fire of Mount Horeb (probably the Deuteronomist's version of Sinai) but saw no form. Moses explains to them that they must take care and not make idols for themselves, in human or animal form, nor worship 'the sun, the moon, and the stars, all the host of heaven' (the angels, Deut. 4.19). Recounting the Ten Commandments, Moses seems to contradict himself and say, 'The LORD spoke with you face to face at the mountain, out of the fire' (Deut. 5.4). But then Moses explains: 'At that time I was standing between the LORD and you to declare to you the words of the LORD; for you were afraid because of the fire and did not go up the mountain' (Deut. 5.5).

Why this distancing? It may be about the problem of idols: the second commandment forbids the making of idols based on anything heavenly or earthly (Ex. 20.4; Deut. 5.8). And this issue has arisen not just in Judaism, but also in Christianity (see below and Chapter 5) and in Islam. It is about much more than simply worshipping a lifeless (and thus gazeless)[4] object that I have made, or that someone else has made. It is about what that object represents, the values and beliefs that I project on to it; quite often it is *myself* that I project. If I and my tribe are aggressive and violent, don't be surprised if we worship a warrior god. And this continues in an apparently atheist society. Worshipping money, sex, beauty ... As we saw, even good, high-minded intentions can become idol worship.

And this may also help to explain the command not to worship the 'the sun, the moon, and the stars, all the host of heaven' (Deut. 4.19). The stars are angels and the angels are stars in Jewish tradition (Job 38.7; Isa. 40.24–26; Bar. 3.34; the apocryphal 1 Enoch; and cf. Rev. 1.20, 8.10–11). Similarly, the fixed stars are living beings in Platonic and Ptolemaic cosmology. The trouble is that some of the angels are fallen (Genesis 6): the devil and his angels who went after women and begot with them the destructive giants; according to the expansion of this story in 1 Enoch (7–8), they taught witchcraft to women and warfare to men. This culminated in the Flood, the destruction of life on earth. The fallen angels offer humankind a false ascent, marked by power-grabbing, selfishness, lust, violence and manipulation – the very same traps that the activist, the doctor, the artist, the mystic and the lover can fall into. At its worst, this is an ascent by black magic: Paul warns the young churches that 'even Satan disguises himself as an angel of light' (2 Cor. 11.14) and reiterates the ban on the worship of angels (Col. 3.18). Ascents – social, political, professional, artistic, romantic and above all spiritual – can be deceptive, and so in itself ascent is ambiguous and *not safe*. That does not mean, of course, that people should be forbidden to ascend, but abuses may have coloured the composition of the biblical narratives (see White 2015, pp. 21, 38, 134–5). Also, the retelling of the story in Deuteronomy may reflect the restoration of the Law and the reordering of the Temple in the reign of King Josiah, during which it was apparently purged of vessels made for the Canaanite Baal and Asherah and the worship of the host of heaven. The priests who had engaged in this worship were deposed (2 Kings 23.1–5; Barker 2003, pp. 148–52; White 2015, pp. 134–5).

Deuteronomy seems to overcome the problem of how God can be seen without people worshipping idols by putting in an intermediary to see God on their behalf. This is the role of Moses when he goes up the mountain (Deut. 5.23–26). The people are afraid of the fire, but they say that 'God may *speak* to someone and the person may still live' (v. 24, my emphasis). They do not mention seeing. In Exodus, Moses ascends the mountain, where he spends 40 days and nights. God shows him how to build the tabernacle and fit it out with the table of the Bread of the Presence, the lampstand and so on; and the Lord tells Moses, 'See that you make them according to the pattern for them, which is being shown you on the mountain' (Ex. 25.40). Moses sees the Lord and his tabernacle/temple.

The earthly temple will be made after the form of the more perfect heavenly temple. The resemblance to Plato's theory of heavenly forms in which earthly particulars participate is very striking (White 2019).

Having received from God the two tablets of the Ten Commandments and detailed instruction about the construction of the tabernacle and worship, Moses came down the mountain only to find that the people are worshipping the golden calf. God forgives the people, but still sends a plague on them (Ex. 32). After speaking with God face to face in the tabernacle, and then not seeing his face when God passes by the cleft in the rock, Moses is called by God to ascend Mount Sinai a second time (but this time alone) with two new tablets of stone for God to write on. God descends in a cloud (Ex. 34.5) and Moses worships, but we are not told that he sees God. However, when Moses comes down the mountain, the skin of his face is shining and people are afraid to come near him. But Moses calls them, and he transmits the commandments and everything God said to him. Then he covers his face with a veil. And after this, whenever Moses goes 'in before the Lord' to speak with him, his face is unveiled, and people see his face shining when he comes out, but then he veils it again until he next goes in to speak with God (Ex. 34.29–35). Of course, the whole people were never able to see God in the first place, but there is a sense that the people have become distanced from God, and that in Deuteronomy the emphasis is away from the vision of God and towards God's voice/Word. This could be because of Aaron's sin, in which the whole people took part. From now on, Moses alone will see God.

When the story is retold in Deuteronomy by Moses, he does not mention that his face was shining (Deut. 10); perhaps this indicates a fear of people idolizing him, as they still try unsuccessfully today to make gods out of their pastors. Deuteronomy does not deny that Moses saw God, but it puts the emphasis more on the voice and hearing, with the obedience that implies, than on seeing. Hence *Shema'*, '*Hear*, O Israel' (Deut. 6.1), one of the most sacred verses in Judaism.

But the people continue to see God's glory reflected in the

face of the high priest, who had entered the Holy of Holies ('When shall I come and behold the face of God?' Ps. 42.2). In the 'deuterocanonical' Book of Sirach (Ecclesiasticus), we read that when Simon, son of Onias, came out from 'the house of the curtain', that is, the Holy of Holies, he is described as 'glorious',

> Like the morning star among the clouds,
> Like the full moon at the festal season,
> Like the sun shining on the temple of the Most High,
> Like the rainbow gleaming in splendid clouds. (Sir. 50.5–7)

What then can we make of 'You cannot see my face; for no one shall see me and live' (Ex. 33.20)? Since *panim* (faces) 'is used to denote a person's presence, and was used outside Israel to denote the "presence" of a deity in an image' (Clements 1972, p. 216; cf. Dozeman 2009, p. 731), did Moses not see God at all, but only his back (Ex. 33.11)? This recalls Levinas's understanding of the face as the way the other person presents themselves (see Chapter 2). But this meaning ultimately rests on the concept of the face. And what, then, does it mean to see God's back?

Or is God's face metaphorical? The tension between apparently seeing God's face but actually only his back is interpreted by Cornelis Houtman (2000, p. 680) to mean that God 'will make an abundant display of his mercy and grace to Moses and therewith guarantee the restoration of the covenant, but who YHWH is in the depth of his being is something that must remain hidden even from Moses'. But is this hiddenness already present in the dazzling aspect of God's face – like the sun for Plato? So bright that we cannot see it fully?

Fear of idolatry could also mean that the vision was sometimes hidden too. Houtman shows that in certain Targums (Aramaic translations of the Hebrew Scriptures made from the first century AD onwards, when Hebrew was no longer spoken by many Jews), 'face to face' is replaced with *mmll (l)qbl mmll*, 'word to word' (Houtman, p. 695). Likewise, in the Neofiti Targum, the blessing of Numbers 6 ('May God ... make his face to shine upon you') is not translated into Aramaic but left in the original Hebrew: 'The Blessing of the Priests [is] read out but not interpreted' (Neofiti Targum, in Mishnah *Megillah* 4.10; see Barker 2010, p. 101). Houtman himself shifts the emphasis from the divine vision to the divine command: Moses has an 'aureole' (that is, halo, Ex. 34.29–35), but only so that 'His radiant external is the visible guarantee that the *laws* he promulgates are in truth YHWH's ordinances' (2000, p. 714, my emphasis). An intriguing suggestion about Moses' mediating role comes from Carol Meyers (2005, p. 267): Moses' radiance indicates the subsuming of his own personality 'into his role as mediator ... to the extent that like God, he must cover his face, the locus of God's presence in him'.

A solution employed by one tradition in Judaism was to say that the vision was not of God but of an angel. In Genesis 33.20 Jacob, having fought God all night, saw his face and called the place *Peni-el*, 'face of God'. But according to another tradition, 'he strove with the *angel* and prevailed' (Hos. 12.4, my emphasis). In the apocryphal Book of Jubilees, a retelling of Genesis around the structure of the Temple feasts, it is the Angel of the Presence who explains the history of Israel to Moses. An angel named Phanuel ('Presence/Face of God') is mentioned in 1 Enoch (40.10, 71.8–9). The priest could be understood as an 'angel' (*mal'ach*), literally, a 'messenger'.

But maybe we do not need to strain too much. The Jewish Platonist Philo of Alexandria, the Judeo-Christian apocryphal text the *Slavonic Apocalypse of Enoch* and the Jewish Merkabah mystics of the New Testament period offer a different angle. While Philo, a contemporary of Jesus, does not comment on Moses' face-to-face (or face-to-back) encounters with God, he reads the story of Moses' death in Deuteronomy 33—34 as being told by Moses himself (the five books of the Pentateuch were traditionally all ascribed to Moses). According to Philo, Moses was taken to immortality, 'summoned thither by the Father Who resolved his twofold nature of soul and body into a single unity, transforming his whole being into mind, pure as the sunlight' (Philo, *Moses*, 288/p. 592).

From the broader context of Philo's writings we might reasonably infer the heavy influence of Neo-Platonism here.

The *Slavonic Apocalypse of Enoch*, commonly known as 2 Enoch, comes through the Slavic Eastern churches but does not really fit easily into any known Jewish or Christian tradition (2 Enoch, pp. 95–97).[5] It relates how the patriarch Enoch is taken up through the heavens (cf. Gen. 5.24), and transformed. And the Merkabah 'Throne' mystic Rabbi Ishmael (first or second century AD?) experienced a transformation not just in himself but in his whole view of creation:

> When my ears heard this great mystery,
> The world was transformed over me in purity

And my heart was as if I had arrived in [a] new world

> Every day it appeared to my soul
> As if I was standing in front of the throne of glory.
> (*Merkavah Rabbah* 680/Schäfer 1982, p. 114)

Commenting on this in the light of Isaiah's vision of the Lord sitting on a throne, Margaret Barker says:

> When the mystic has stood before the throne and seen the presence of the Lord, he [or she] sees everything else differently. After he had seen the Lord, Isaiah learned that his glory filled the whole creation. The blessing of the high priests linked seeing the face with the gifts of wisdom, grace and peace [Num 6:24–26], and a saying attributed to Rabbi Ishmael shows how this altered perception of the whole world was central to the *merakavah* tradition.
>
> This describes his new way of being in the world: he stands before the throne, and sees the creation as the Creator sees it. (Barker 2010, pp. 105–6)

The implication for Philo's account of Moses' death is that, in a sense, Moses had already 'died' and was transformed when he saw God face to face. This is why we cannot see God and live. But for those willing to die, the reward is very great.

And in Rabbi Ishmael's understanding, the change in how

we view creation must apply especially to how we see others, since the Word of God has already taught us that God made humankind, male and female, in his own image (Gen. 1.26). So following on from our philosophical investigations in Chapter 2, the purifying vision of God means that we die to gazing on the other as a mere projection of desire (Lacan, Mulvey), or scrutinizing them according to 'norms' of the healthy/beautiful body and behaviour (the clinical and surveillance gaze as described by Foucault, re-read in the light of digital culture). My gaze is purified of the self-centred ontologies I have constructed. All these noxious gazes have to die, so that I can see the face of the other, and see the reality (see Chapter 2, on Levinas). 'Look to him, and be radiant, so your faces shall never be ashamed' (Ps. 34.5). Indeed, we look differently not just at other human beings but at the whole creation. We cease to be anthropocentric, and there is an effect – think of Saint Francis and the animals ...

But we have still not solved the problem of Moses being able to see only God's back. Let's turn to Gregory of Nyssa (fourth century), with a glance at Augustine (fifth century). I appreciate that for some readers it is too easy for Christians to project their interpretations on to the Hebrew Scriptures rather than reading them on their own terms. But Gregory and Augustine are more careful than this, and in any case we are already seeing a theme of death and resurrection emerging, which supports the view of a Rabbi friend of mine that 'Christianity is a direction Judaism could have gone'.

So according to Gregory, Scripture is telling us through Moses' two experiences of God that the ascent of the spiritual life is also a two-stage process. First, through a similar process of purification, we ascend the mountain of knowledge, escaping the darkness of this world, experiencing religious knowledge at first as light. Later we 'enter into the darkness where God is' and participate in the light, then see more clearly 'what of the divine nature is uncontemplated' (Gregory of Nyssa, *Life of Moses* 152/p. 91, 162/p. 95), that is, what is beyond senses and intelligence. He is going further than Plato – the voice of God is shown not to be contradicting the vision, but presenting it: the Divine Word forbids that the Divine be likened to any things known to humankind (Gregory, 165/ pp. 95–6). Boldly, he argues that the unbearable brightness of Moses' transformation anticipates the Second Coming of Christ (217–218/p. 111).

Gregory says that the contradiction of the face-to-face vision and then God allowing only a face-to-back vision cannot be read literally, because it leads to an inappropriate concept of God: front and back pertain to a shape, and a shape to a body, and God is incorruptible and incorporeal. Instead, Gregory sees this as belonging to Moses' spiritual ascent (arguing that only a spiritual reading will make sense of the passage):

> He shone with glory. And although lifted up through such lofty experiences, he is still unsatisfied in his desire for more. He still thirsts for that with which he constantly filled himself to capacity, and he asks to attain as if he had never partaken, beseeching God to appear to him, not according to his capacity to partake, but according to God's true being. (230/p. 114)

The divine voice 'granted what was requested in what was denied, showing in a few words an immeasurable depth of thought'. God granted the fulfilment of Moses' desire, but didn't promise that this desire would stop or be satisfied. What Moses wants – God himself – is precisely what leaves his desire unsatisfied: God is beyond all characteristics (232–235/p. 115). Indeed, to die is for desire to cease, so in that respect, Gregory argues, humankind cannot see God and live. He reads the place, the rock in which God says he will hide Moses (Ex. 33.21–22), as Christ: 'the heavenly places' (Eph. 1.3); 'Christ ... in whom are *hidden* all the treasures of wisdom and knowledge' (Col. 2.2–3, my emphasis). We are *followers* of Jesus, he is leading us – and you see not the front of your guide but his back. Augustine says that Exodus 33.12–23 specifically refers to Christ, because although God tells Moses he will hide him in the rock and let him see his back, Scripture does not record that this actually happened to Moses – it is only fulfilled when

Christ, the Messiah, appears (Augustine, *Questions on the Heptateuch*, II.154.7–8/pp. 166–7).[6]

The initial experience of receiving the face of the other is a conversion of heart: for the first time, we see the other. Yet this is not the end: it is only the beginning of a relationship by which the Divine Word will progressively break the idols that we make of the other person and of creation. As Timothy Radcliffe said to me, we start in a friendship with what we have in common (what is like me – even if the other person's difference attracts me, it is because this difference is something that I want for myself). The challenge comes when we find how we are different (in a way that I don't like). Will we then see them as they are, embrace their otherness, and continue on this journey?

And this is all the more important because we believe that the other is made in God's image and likeness, which means that since each person is unique, each person gives me a unique view on God. And at the same time I can never worship the other person as God, because that would be to see neither God nor the person – indeed, it would put an unreasonable demand on them, a demand that so often leads to the breakdown of a relationship. Bringing together Plato's ascent of the lover with Scripture, Gregory of Nyssa says of Moses' shining with the divine glory and yet longing for more:

> Such an experience seems to me to belong to the soul which loves what is beautiful. Hope always draws the soul from the beauty which is seen to what is beyond, always kindles the desire for the hidden through what is constantly perceived. Therefore, the ardent lover of beauty, although receiving what is always visible as an image of what he desires, yet longs to be filled with the very stamp of the archetype. (*Life of Moses*, 231/p. 114)

What is beyond, what is hidden ... We shine with the reflection of the one we love, yet our desire is for what is beyond our sight, what is (as yet) hidden, and there will always be more.

Jesus: God's divinizing gaze

Seeing

The vision of God is fulfilled in the New Testament: 'Whoever has seen me has seen the Father' (John 14.9). Peter, James, and John, Jesus' inner circle, saw him transfigured: according to Mark (9.3), his clothes turned a dazzling white; according to Matthew, his face also shone like the sun (Matt. 17.2), while Luke says that the appearance of his face changed (literally, 'became *other*' – we will return to this) and his clothes became dazzling white (Luke 9.29).

Modern biblical commentaries do not have much to say about Jesus' gaze. His seeing and looking at others just seem to be a natural part of his being human. But the *Catena Aurea* (CA), a digest of patristic commentary on the Gospels compiled by St Thomas Aquinas in the thirteenth century, often reflects on the gaze of God made human in Jesus, so I will make special use of it, not least because some of Aquinas' sources are now lost (such as Alcuin, a seventh-century monk, and Remigius, a missionary and bishop, *c.* 437–533).[7]

A prime example is Jesus' calling of Simon and Andrew when they are fishing in Lake Galilee (Matt. 4.18). Remigius says that Jesus '*saw*, that is, not so much with the bodily eye, as spiritually viewing their hearts' (CA vol. 1, pp. 135–6). Similarly, when Jesus sees Nathanael coming to him he says, 'I saw you under the fig tree before Philip called you' (John 1.48). John Chrysostom comments that Jesus saw him 'not having beheld him as man, but as God discerning him from above' (CA vol. 4, p. 76).[8]

This reflects more than just a high Christology: the verb used for 'to see', here and in most other places in the New Testament, is *horao*, a 'defective' verb made up from different stems. The aorist (for our purposes, past historic tense) is *eidon*, from the same root as *oida*, 'I know': to have seen is to know. Jesus' seeing moves him to compassion for the crowd he recognizes as distressed and 'like sheep without a shepherd' (Matt. 9.36, cf. Matt. 14.14). And when he approaches Jerusalem he weeps over it and says, 'If you, even you, had only recognized (literally, 'known', *egnos*) on this day the things that make for peace! But they are hidden from your eyes.' Jesus sees and thus knows: but the city doesn't see, and therefore doesn't know. Jesus' gaze is a cinematic gaze of depth. Not voyeuristic, or controlling, or judgemental, but seeing the significance where others see only the surface.

Jesus promises Nathanael that he will see heaven opened and angels ascending and descending on the Son of Man (John 1.51). 'See how He raises him from earth for a while, and forces [original, 'causes'] him to think that Christ is not a mere man ... It was, as it were, saying that He was Lord of the Angels' (CA vol. 4, p. 76; John Chrysostom, *Homilies on the Gospel of John*, xxi.1/p. 73). Jesus' seeing of Nathanael is not a surveying or clinical gaze. It means that Nathanael will see more, will be raised up when he sees who Jesus really is. 'Angels ascending and descending' of course recalls Jacob's vision of the ladder and God revealing himself to Jacob as 'the Lord', at the place that he called 'the house of God and the gate of heaven' (Gen. 28.17). Later, Jacob will fight God/the angel of God all night, and be rewarded with the face-to-face vision of God. Often fighting God is part of our relationship with him. We project on to him everything we hate about ourselves. Perhaps this is why lovers sometimes fight. Sometimes it is part of a spiritual purification, as when the exhausted Psalmist begs God to turn his face away from him (Ps. 39.13). But it seems there is no fight between Jesus and Nathanael, 'in whom there is no deceit' (John 1.47). Rather, the pure-hearted Nathanael not only hears the Lord, the Son of God (John 1.49), but sees him face to face.

A further level in the verb 'to see' is in the future tense form of *horao*, which is *opsomai* and 'middle': as we saw earlier, this is neither active nor passive, but has a reflexive and often reciprocal, relational sense. It may be objected that this is a coincidence arising from the translation of Jesus' words, which were probably spoken in Aramaic. But the middle voice is carried in the meaning of Jesus' teaching: 'Blessed are the pure of heart, for they shall see God [*opsontai*]' (Matt 5.8) – they shall see God and God will see them. Indeed, we shall see ourselves, and in seeing God, St John says, 'we shall be like him, for we will see [*opsometha*] him as he is' (1 John 3.2).

So in John 16.22, Jesus says, 'So you have pain now; but I will see you [*opsomai hymas*] again, and your hearts will rejoice, and no one will take your joy from you.' Alcuin exactly grasps the reciprocity/reflexivity of this gaze: 'i.e. I will take you to *myself*. Or, *I will see you again*, i.e. I shall appear again, *and be seen by you*; and your heart shall rejoice' (CA vol. 6, p. 514, my emphasis).

When Jesus sees Levi the tax collector (Luke 5.27), the verb is *etheasato*, 'contemplate', which we have already encountered in Plato. It is an active receptivity. On the level of human encounter with the divine, because God lovingly beholds me and I am graced to see him, I become myself. Likewise, in John's Gospel, when two disciples of John the Baptist hear from their master that Jesus is the Lamb of God who takes away the sins of the world and turn and follow Jesus, he turns round and gazes at them (*theasamenos*): as John McHugh (2009, p. 136) says, a 'beholding ... with the physical eyes, but in such a way that a supernatural impression is gained'. The disciples ask Jesus ('Rabbi') where he is staying and he invites them to come and see.

Blessed Theophylact (Bishop of Ohrid, *c.* 1050–after 1107) comments:

> If you do not follow Jesus by means of good actions, you will not attain the vision of the Lord's countenance, nor will you come to His dwelling place, that is, reach the enlightenment of divine knowledge. (CA vol. 4, p. 67; Theophylact, *The Explanation of the Holy Gospel According to John*, p. 34)

Theophylact in particular stresses ethical behaviour as the precondition of the divine vision; note how Enoch the visionary was 'righteous' (1 Enoch 1.2, 12.4, 15.1), just as for Levinas ethics preceded ontology.

According to Alcuin,

> [t]he disciples followed behind His back in order to see Him, and did not see His face. So He turns round, and, as it were, lowers His majesty, that they might be enabled to behold His face. (CA vol. 4, p. 67)

Theophylact and Alcuin have seen the connection with Moses that we explored above – seeing the Lord's back because we are following the Lord as guide. And now the ministry of Moses, whose shining face showed the glory of God to the people, is fulfilled in Jesus, the great High Priest who is God.

Catherine Pickstock compares with the middle voice the mediating priesthood of the 'ineffably divine and human' Christ, and by extension the saints and those who are anointed to represent him ministerially on earth (Pickstock 1998, p. 157). This is a middle voice that does not separate the individual from God, but actually connects us with God and with one another through the kinship of Church and its extension into Christian society (pp. 155–7). Another observation of Pickstock's about the 'middle voice' could well be applied to the extraordinary reciprocity of God's gaze in Jesus:

> The two movements of receiving and passing on are mutually constitutive and perhaps one could add that the act of receiving is indistinguishable from, or is itself, a counter-gift of return. Such circulation of gift is only possible in a theological order genuinely spoken in the middle voice, an wholly other mode which authentically outwits the shuttling between action and passion of the secular order. (Pickstock, p. 112)

Historically, theologians have had some trouble with the idea of God being able to be receptive. Receptivity was regarded as passive, whereas God, according to Aquinas, is pure act (*Summa Theologiae*, Ia 9.1), in the sense that God is fully real: there is no unrealized potential in God. But this does not entail receptivity, as indicating God's need to receive something that makes him complete; and therefore receptivity is incompatible with the Divine Nature. Stratford Caldecott draws out the very serious consequences of this mistake:

> The tradition that God, being pure act, contained no trace of passivity had become associated with the tendency in Catholic and Christian thought to assign a lower place to woman and to 'feminine' virtues. In a society that increasingly valued the hard, driving mechanisms of technological progress and economic competition, theology became entangled with the same attitude. According to [Hans Urs von] Balthasar, on the other hand, to *receive something from another* is not at all a weakness or imperfection, but intrinsic to the nature of what it is to love. This meant that theology was free to revalue the feminine – and the child. Balthasar's theology is thus closely allied with the 'alternative' stream of affective and mystical theology flowing through feminine mystics from Teresa of Avila and Margaret Mary Alocoque to Thérèse of Lisieux and her 'Little Way' of spiritual childhood. (Balthasar himself was so closely associated with the mystic Adrienne von Speyr that he claimed their works could never be separated.) (Caldecott 2013, p. 258 n. 12).[9]

Small wonder if we have ended up with a culturally common image of God as a distant, exclusively male figure with a Foucaultian gaze of surveillance. But man *and woman* were made equal and different in God's image and likeness, together, in the encounter of faces.

Looking

When Jesus looks, generally two verbs are used, based on *blepo* ('look'). One is *emblepo*, 'look *into*'. Jesus doesn't just look vaguely in someone's direction because he wants something or that person is talking to him. As we have already seen, Jesus' depth gaze is not a clinical or surveying gaze, but a gaze that loves with a love that may include an element of challenge, because it may reveal uncomfortable truths. So Jesus looks at Simon Peter and sees who Peter truly is: '[Andrew] brought Simon to Jesus, who looked at him and said, "You are Simon son of John. You are to be called Cephas"' (Aramaic for *petros*, rock, hence Peter) (John 1.42). As St Bede comments, Jesus 'beheld' Peter 'not with his natural eye only, but by the insight of His Godhead discerned from eternity the simplicity and greatness of his soul, for which he was to be elevated above the whole Church' (CA vol. 4, p. 10). Unlikely though Peter's frailty makes this, he is revealed as a rock when he is transformed by the divine gaze. As with ourselves, Peter's true nature is not realized all at once: Jesus looks at Peter during his passion, and Peter remembers Jesus' prediction that he would deny him three times (Luke 22.61).

Jesus' gaze can be challenging too: the divine gaze purges away all that is not good, not of God. So he looked at the law-abiding rich young man and loved him, and said: 'You lack one thing; go, sell what you own, and give the money to the poor, and you will have treasure in heaven; then come, follow me' (Mark 10.21). But he looks around (*periblepsamenos*) at his less wealthy disciples and says: 'How hard it will be for those who have wealth to enter the kingdom of God' (Mark 10.23; cf. Mark 3.5). Yet he challenges them too, because he looks at them and says, 'With mortals it is impossible, but not for God; for God all things are possible' (Mark 10.27).

Jesus turns his eyes *towards* the crowd when he reveals the Beatitudes to them (Luke 6.20) – but the Greek has the sense not just of turning towards but also of exaltation. St Ambrose says, 'But being about to utter His divine oracles, He begins to rise higher; although He stood in a low place, yet as it is said, *He lifted up his eyes*. What is lifting up the eyes, but to disclose a more hidden light?' (CA vol. 3, p. 208). The consummation of the Platonic ascent.

Unsurprisingly, Jesus lifts up his eyes (*eparas tous ophthalmous autou*) to heaven when, on the eve of his Passion, he prayed to his heavenly Father for glorification (John 17.1). And this too was for his disciples' benefit: John Chrysostom says, 'He lifted up his eyes to heaven to teach us intentness in our prayers: that we should stand with uplifted eyes, not of the body only, but of the mind' (CA vol. 4, pp. 522–3, St John Chrysostom, Homily lxxx.1/p. 296;[10] cf. Col. 3.2). John Chrysostom reminds us of the 'embodied sacred'[11] – in looking upwards, we are raised to the highest spirituality, the journey to the face-to-face vision of God. John the Evangelist sees the heavenly worship (Rev. 4.1), and Paul clearly has in mind Moses' face-to-face encounter with God when he says,

> For now we see [literally look, *blepomen*] in a mirror, dimly, but then we will see [no verb in original] face to face. Now I know only in part; then I will know fully, even as I have been fully known. (1 Cor. 13.12)

Like a mirror – seeing and being seen. We will see God and know him and, in his gaze, be fully known. What is implied is transformation, 'becoming *other*' like Jesus in his Transfiguration, not just into the likeness of an angel, as per Enoch, but into the likeness of God himself. And then be fully known as ourselves:

> Beloved, we are God's children now; what we will be has not yet been revealed. What we do know is this: when he is revealed, we will be like him, for we will see [*opsometha*] him as he is. (1 John 3.2)

Seeing the face of God and being seen by him, the servants of God and the Lamb will have the divine Name on their foreheads and 'need no light of lamp or sun, for the Lord God will be their light, and they will reign for ever and ever' (Rev. 22.5). We will explore this more in the next chapter.

But first, what does Jesus teach about how we should gaze in everyday life, the ethical beginning and precondition for the divine vision?

Jesus' teaching on the gaze

From his own seeing and looking, Jesus teaches his audiences. Terrifyingly, he tells his hearers to tear out their eye if it causes them to gaze with the covetous, lustful gaze (Matt. 5.27–28). This is because, as Ola Sigurdson says (2016, p. 189), the eye is the lamp of the body, a metaphor in Judaism for a person's character. In other words, how I look, the shine of my gaze, reveals who I am. Tearing out the eye can be seen as a call to root-and-branch reform of one's character. And this is something only God can do. In the ancient world, the eyewitness was not a disconnected bystander, but a participant in the action (p. 195). If people see our good works, they will give glory to God (Matt. 5.16); because they see God working through us, they see us acting divinely. Those who are pure of heart gaze generously, because they see God at work, just as in Jesus they see the Father (John 3.31–32, 5.19–20, 14.17).

Thus Simeon can say that he has *seen* the Lord's salvation (Luke 2.27). This also shows the significance of Jesus' miraculous healing of the blind: they can then see and take part. Of course, many have seen but don't believe (whereas Brother Vince, a blind Dominican I was privileged to live with, saw God better than many of us). When Jesus heals Bar Timaeus, while still blind the man recognizes him as the Son of David (and the crowds try to silence him): when he receives his sight, he follows Jesus (Mark 10.46–52).

But Jesus complains to the crowd that, unlike the blind man, they have seen him (*heorakete*) yet do not believe (John 6.36). But those who gaze on the Son (with a sense of contemplation, *theoron*) and believe in him will have eternal life (6.40). Because the world has not gazed on Jesus, it cannot receive the Spirit. But Mary Magdalene, first witness of the Resurrection, gazed on the Lord (*theorei*, John 21.14), and therefore can say that she has seen (*heoraka*) the Lord (John 21.18) (Sigurdson 2016, pp. 202–3). In the next world, of course, the seeing will be mutual, *ospesthe*, the middle voice, because we will be sharing fully in the divine nature.

But even now not just our actions but our gaze may mediate Christ's gaze. A gaze by Jesus that we might well miss, but that will prove central to understanding how Christians should gaze, is noticed by Fabrice Hadjadj. A contemporary French Catholic thinker of Tunisian Jewish/Muslim parentage, Hadjadj was an atheist for many years before his conversion. His views on the graced possibilities of the gaze are revolutionary:

> The Lord is there and does not say, 'Look at me,' but, 'Look at the lilies of the field' ... The Word of God does not trample on creation, but rather, under his gaze of love, it appears in a dignity which is greater than royalty. (Hadjadj 2012, p. 61; cf. Matt. 6.28; Luke 12.27)

Jesus' looking is not one of clinical diagnosis or surveillance, let alone a gaze of erotic consumption, but he looks in a way that actually draws the attention away from himself, while glorifying whatever he is looking at, showing it as it really is. The lilies appear in glory when Jesus casts his gaze of divine love on them – just as Jesus' appearance 'was made other' in his Transfiguration and he was revealed in his dazzling glory (Luke 9.29; Sigurdson 2016, p. 188).

With regard to the lilies, Jesus actually says 'consider' (*katamathete*, Matt. 6.28; *katanoesate*, 'come to know', Luke 12.27). But clearly one cannot consider without looking, seeing, beholding. Quite clearly, this shows us that God's glory is present in creation – we should not fear becoming pagans if as Christians we find the spiritual in nature. It is an act of receiving rather than projection. As brothers and sisters of Christ, imitating him, we are given grace to see and to look as Christ sees – to see and love the glory in each and every person as uniquely made in the image and likeness of God (Gen. 1.27), to reveal that divine image in the other person and, like Rabbi Ishmael, to see the glory in the whole of creation.

Yet at every moment this gaze demands that we die to power-grabbing and idolatry, which, as we saw at the beginning of this chapter, can derail the most admirable visions. It keeps our gaze loving, the gaze of God made flesh in Jesus that fulfils and surpasses the still impersonal and chilly Platonic vision of the height of beauty. This gaze is the healing grace of Christ for the wound of the image, the wound epitomized by the doctored selfie.

But the challenge for us Christians is that unlike Peter, Andrew, Nathanael and even the rich young man and the Pharisees, we no longer see Jesus face to face. Now, in the time of the Church, we see 'dimly as in a mirror'. What does that mean for us – and for those people whose first contact with Jesus will probably be the face of a Christian? How (well) have we learned to gaze, and how has Christian tradition envisioned and shown Jesus' gaze? We will explore this over the next two chapters.

Notes

1 Martin Earle, an artist, said this to me with regard to contemplation.

2 Note that in Latin *altus* can mean both 'deep' and 'high'.

3 Hebrew is written in consonants, which are pointed with the addition of vowels by the reader/interpreter. So the consonant stem *yr'h* means 'see'. With the prefix *w-* it is past/narrative tense. Pointed *wayyira'u* (Qal), it means 'they saw', but as *wayyera'u* (Niph'al), it means 'they appeared/presented themselves/were seen'. My thanks to Margaret Barker for this elucidation.

4 I am indebted to M. C. Benitan for this observation.

5 Not to be confused with *The Hebrew Apocalypse of Enoch*, or 3 Enoch, a Merkabah/Hekhalot text probably dating to the fifth century of our era.

6 The closest is when God manifests himself to Elijah, having commanded Elijah to go and stand on the mountain. With all the earthquake, wind and fire, it is not surprising that Elijah hides himself in a cave, from which he emerges on hearing the silence, or still small voice (1 Kings 19.11–14).

7 As Aidan Nichols points out in his introduction to the 1997 reprint, although not all quotations are correctly ascribed, and where they are traceable Aquinas often paraphrases rather than quotes verbatim, CA reflects a particularly symbolic and preaching-orientated approach to the Gospels (CA vol. 1, pp. v–vi, ix). CA also preserves the lost material from Alcuin and Remigius (see Newman's preface, p. viii).

8 In the original, 'He still enquired as of a man, but Jesus answers as God' (John Chrysostom, *Homilies on the Gospel of John*, xx.2, p. 71).

9 See also McCabe 1987.

10 Aquinas paraphrases the section, but is true to the spirit of it.

11 I am indebted to Veronika Hliničanova for this expression.

5

Gazes of the Early Church

After Jesus had ascended into heaven, his Body the Church would become people's main experience of the divine gaze. Exploring the history of the Church, we shall see good gazes and bad gazes, but also hopefully some resources to deepen our understanding of gazing divinely.

The vision of Stephen: no one can see God and live

The gaze of the first Christians was both a gaze into heaven and the healing gaze of God on others. The stern preaching of Stephen, revealing the hardheartedness of his hearers, is blessed by God with a vision of Christ in heaven which, through words, Stephen shares with his audience. During his trial, the council members gazed intently at Stephen (Acts 6.15). The Greek (*atenisantes*) suggests an intent or hard, unbending gaze. They saw (*eidon*) that his face was like the face of an angel. This is because he is reflecting the divine glory, transformed in God's presence like Enoch, whose face also shone like the face of an angel.[1] Then Stephen gazed intently (*atenisas*) into heaven and he saw (*eiden*) the glory of God. He mediates this vision to his hearers through words:

> Look ... I see [*idou theoro*, literally 'behold' or 'contemplate'] the heavens opened and the Son of Man standing at the right hand of God! (Acts 7.56)

We saw in the last chapter the controversies in ancient Israel around seeing the face of God, and the ban on explaining the meaning of the blessing in Numbers 6.25 ('The LORD make his face to shine upon you'). So maybe it is no surprise that when Stephen told his angry audience of his vision, they covered their ears, and put him to death (Acts 7.54–60). No one can see God and live, indeed ...[2]

Before Stephen's martyrdom, Acts also narrates how Peter and John healed a lame man outside the Temple. Peter and John looked intently at him (*atenisas* again), and Peter tells him to look at them (*blepson*). The mutual gaze. Then Peter says, 'In the name of Jesus Christ of Nazareth, stand up and walk' (Acts 3.6). And the man is healed (Acts 3.1–7).

Timothy Radcliffe comments on the intensity of this mutual gaze:

> This reciprocal gaze embodies Israel's deepest longing that God might look at her graciously and she might look at God. 'Let your face shine on us and we shall be saved' (Psalm 80.3). In the First Eucharistic Prayer we ask, in a slightly strange translation, that God will look at us 'with a serene and kindly countenance.' We want to be smiled at. Madonna, the British singer, begs: 'Jesus Christ will you look at me/ Don't know who I's supposed to be.' (Radcliffe 2019, p. 288, citing Roman Missal p. 675; cf. Brown 2007, pp. 303 and 307)

Peter and John look on the lame man with the gaze of Christ, the divine gaze. Their gaze *is* God's gaze on others because they have been transformed by Christ's gaze. The reference to the Name is no coincidence. In Revelation John says, 'they will see his face, and his *name* will be on their foreheads' (Rev. 22.4, my emphasis).

And as we have already seen in the last chapter, in 1 John 3.2, we will be fulfilled because we have become like God.

> Beloved, we are God's children now; what we will be has not yet been revealed. What we do know is this: when he is revealed, we will be like him, for we will see [*opsometha*] him as he is. (1 John 3.2)

This is the fruit of dying with Christ to rise to our true identity: it is nothing less than divinization. In 2 Peter 1.4 we read that through God's gifts to us, especially his knowledge, God has given us his promises, so that we 'may become participants in the divine nature [*theias koinonoi physeos*]'. Beautifully, the words are ordered so that 'participants' is right in the middle of the divine nature. *Koinonoi* is connected to *koinonia*, 'fellowship', the communion of the Church (for example, Acts 2.42). Our communion is made through participation in the divine nature. We see Christ in one another: we are transformed and transforming.

Paul compares the status of Christians now with the Jews needing Moses to veil his face on coming down from the mountain (Ex. 34.29–35; see Chapter 2), as the light of God's glory was too bright for them. The people's minds (*noemata* = perceptions, thoughts) were hardened, says Paul. In other words, there was a lack of receptivity. And this was only gazing at the end (*telos*) of a glory that was being set aside. Is there a hint here of the end, that is, the purpose, of that glory – that is, Christ? Moses was to see Christ's back, a prophecy, Augustine said, not fulfilled in the Old Testament (Augustine, *Questions on the Heptateuch*, II.154.7–8/pp. 166–7, see Chapter 4). But

> all of us, with unveiled faces, seeing the glory of the Lord as though reflected in a mirror, are being transformed into the same image from one degree of glory to another; for this comes from the Lord, the Spirit. (2 Cor. 3.18)

What was a secret of the priesthood in the Old Testament is now given to all who are a royal priesthood in Christ (1 Pet. 2.9). Our creation in the image and likeness of God (Gen. 1.26–27) is being fulfilled by grace in a way that we could never imagine. Do Christians actually see God? C. K. Barrett believes that the direct vision of God is only for the next life (Barrett 1973, p. 125), and for most Christians on this earth that will probably be the case. As Paul says, God has shone in our *hearts* 'to give the light of the knowledge of the glory of God in the face of Jesus Christ' (2 Cor. 4.6). 'For now we see [literally look, *blepomen*] in a mirror, dimly, but then we will see face to face. Now I know only in part; then I will know fully, even as I have been fully known' (1 Cor. 13.12).

While Barrett links the transformation of the believer into the image of God with 'the light of the knowledge of the glory of God *in the face* of Jesus Christ' in 2 Corinthians 4.6 (Barrett 1973, p. 125), he insists that the transformation described by Paul 'is not properly mystical; the believer remains distinct from God ... not deified but *transformed into the same image*, the glory they share with him ever increasing' (p. 125). But that is the wonder. The mystic is not subsumed into God, but becomes his or her radiantly beautiful self in God. As in a mirror, we see God in whose image we are made and therefore at last see ourselves. The word for image is *eikona*, whence 'icon'.

St Thomas Aquinas, commenting on 2 Corinthians 3.18, remarks that we behold God (*speculamur*, literally 'mirror'):

> when we rise from a consideration of ourselves to some knowledge of God, and we are transformed. For since all knowledge involves the knower's being assimilated into the thing known, it is necessary that those who see be in some way transformed into God. If they see perfectly, they are perfectly transformed ... 'when he appears we shall be like him' (1 John 3.2) ... 'now we see in a mirror dimly' (1 Cor. 13.12). (*Commentary on 2 Corinthians*, C.3.L.3, p. 445)

And this is not just the influence of Aquinas' epistemology (philosophy of knowledge). It is the convergence of philosophy of knowledge and philosophies of the gaze and of vision with the mystery of the Holy of Holies (see Chapter 4), fulfilled in the revelation of Jesus Christ. Here is the fulfilment of all philosophy that contemplates rather than controls.

And for the early Christians this may not have been just an idea from Paul, a concept communicated with words, but actually a recalling of their own experience of baptism.

Baptism: a ritual of the gaze?

Could Paul's reference in 2 Corinthians 3.18 to 'unveiled faces, seeing the glory of the Lord as though reflected in a mirror' be a memory of the baptismal liturgy? We cannot reconstruct with any certainty the liturgies of the first Christians. But there are what philosopher Ludwig Wittgenstein calls 'family resemblances' between passages in the New Testament, the early Church Fathers, early liturgical constitutions and early Christian art and architecture (Jensen 2011), which taken together build a common picture of a baptismal rite. According to the *Apostolic Tradition* (21–26), if catechumens, candidates for baptism, had passed the test of practical charity (seeing God in the other person) they were to be baptized at cock-crow. Logically, this would mean that when they went from their baptism to join the rest of the community at the Eucharist, it would be sunrise. Vigil was kept through the night, as is still the case in many churches at Easter. The Second Letter of Peter, which we have already cited in relation to 'sharing in the divine nature', may not be an actual transcript of a baptismal liturgy (Kelly 1969, pp. 16–20), but it may well be a sermon to the newly baptized: the allusion to confirming 'your call and election' (2 Pet. 1.10) and, above all, 'You will do well to be attentive to this [the prophetic message] as to a *lamp shining in a dark place, until the day dawns and the morning star rises in your hearts*' (2 Pet. 1.19, my emphasis). Justin Martyr (d. 165) describes the baptismal bath as 'enlightenment' or 'illumination' (*First Apology*, 61/p. 67). Is the gaze on the sunrise? When John saw the Lord in glory, his face 'was like the sun shining with full force' (Rev. 1.16).

To some this reconstruction may seem fanciful, a projection back on to the early Church of liturgies formed down the centuries. But we have had centuries of reading word as metaphor, against concrete, somatic reality. Baptism *is* very somatic in the New Testament: baptism was by immersion, following Jewish custom (as in the baptism of John the Baptist, and to this day the Jewish *miqveh* or ritual bath), so the newly baptized were quite literally 'raised up' out of the water (Col. 3.1). They had put off the old self, put to death sin in the stripping off of clothes before entering the baptismal bath (Col. 3.9). Furthermore, when they emerged from the bath, the candidates were anointed with scented oil – if not on their whole bodies, then at least always on their faces – before being clothed in a white robe (see Jensen 2011, pp. 168–75, 234). Jesus was the Messiah, the *Christos* – that is, the 'Anointed One' (cf. Eph. 1.9). John tells a church that they in turn have all 'been anointed by the Holy One, and you all have knowledge' or 'you know all things' (1 John 2.20) – the anointing teaches them all things (1 John 2.27). In the last chapter we saw that Rabbi Ishmael said, 'The world was transformed over me in purity' (*Merkavah Rabbah* 680/Schäfer 1982, p. 114). Some of this sense of purity would undoubtedly come to the newly baptized through the experience of cleansing and the touch and scent of the anointing oil. Including the sense, dare I say, of being loved. And perhaps we can apply to the new Christians what Margaret Barker says of Rabbi Ishmael: they received an 'altered perception of the whole world' (Barker 2010, p. 106).

So they were anointed to be like Jesus. Certainly the bright white robe, recalling Jesus' Transfiguration, would be a sign that in the Lord they were light (Eph. 5.8, cf. Jensen 2011, p. 170); but the oil especially would make their faces shine. Furthermore, when the new Christians entered the main assembly for the dawn Eucharist, if there was a lamp shining there – 'a lamp shining in a dark place, until the day dawns and the morning star rises in your hearts', in the words of 2 Peter – the light would shine on the faces of the baptized. As their faces were already shining with the oil, to anyone seeing them they would be dazzling bright, even as John saw the face of the Lord 'like the sun shining with full force'. The assembly would see the divine image in the face of the newly baptized. And furthermore, these new Christians would see the gaze of those who were looking at them. They would see, from the gaze of others, that they themselves were indeed made in the image and likeness of God. This is the redemption of those traumatic experiences of seeing ourselves being seen that lie at the foundation of Lacan's philosophy and psychoanalysis of the gaze (see Chapter 2).

To this day we speak of people 'shining', and in fact many types of make-up, whether for just the face or for the whole body, contain a shining material (sometimes actual gold) to cover up wrinkles and make the person look younger. Radiant people look more optimistic, positive, always fresh, shining like a star to others.[3] Paul urged the Philippians to 'shine like stars in the world' (Phil. 2.15), like the stars they may well have seen above their heads during the baptismal ritual, as in the baptistery of Dura-Europus (Jensen 2011, pp. 269–70; White 2015, pp. 67–72).

Have we unconsciously made our exegesis and thus our liturgical practice too logocentric, and thus lost the embodied sacred – that embodied sacred that includes seeing, with radiant faces, the presence of God reflected in the other's face? For Cyril of Alexandria (*c.* 370–444), it is in fact the shining of the light of the Only-begotten on to us that transforms us into the Word, the Logos. Through the somatic experience of baptism, we are recreated – including our words (Cyril of Alexandria, *Commentary on the Second Letter to the Corinthians* 5.5).

There lies an opportunity for Christians. We saw in Chapter 1 how make-up has gone beyond what you see in real life, and that the camera's view on social media now *is* real life for many people, and so that's what they need to look like off-camera. It involves a huge amount of make-up and time. But now we have rediscovered what we might call 'the baptismal gaze' of the real face displaying the real me with the aid of oil and light, and being seen as such – radiating the perfection of the true self Christ has saved us to be, unaided by a camera. Surely now is the moment to restore this?

Of course the first Christians, fragile human beings like us, could and did fail in the face of life's trials and in some cases forgot and fell away. Paul complains about the morals of the Corinthians: 'for some people have no knowledge of God. I say this to your shame' (1 Cor. 15.34), and some of the Hebrew Christians were neglecting to meet together (Heb. 10.25). But the memory can always be easily recalled – as in Paul's reminders to the Romans (6.1–14) and Colossians (3.9–10), because of the power of a somatic experience. But we cannot recall what we have not experienced. I, like most Christians today, was baptized as a baby, for which I'm truly grateful – 'Let the little children come to me' (Matt. 19.14). But I don't remember it. And while some churches practise baptism by immersion, in most cases it's just three splashes of water and a couple of dabs of oil, even for adults. In the final chapter we will think more about how we might return to the experience of our baptism.

Part of the challenge of living out our baptism is that although we are baptized we haven't yet arrived at heaven. We can of course forget and fall away, and the trials of life can get us down. But the memory can always be easily recalled – as in Paul's reminders to the Romans (6.1–14) and Colossians (3.9–10), because of the power of a somatic experience.

Of course, part of the challenge of living out their baptism was that the new Christians hadn't arrived at heaven yet. This was only the beginning of their following of Christ in his ascent through the heavens (cf. Eph. 4). Paul celebrates the baptism of the Roman Christians, 'buried with him by baptism into death, so that, just as Christ was raised from the dead by the glory of the Father, so we too might walk in newness of life' (Rom. 6.5). But now there is the problem that we carry on sinning, that we carry on feeling our weakness, Paul as much as anyone else (Rom. 6—7). Quarrels and divisions beset the churches, which Paul tries to sort out in Corinth. The solution is the Law of the Spirit (Rom. 8), and according to Irenaeus, drawing on Ptolemaic cosmology of seven heavens surrounding the earth, each heaven corresponds to a particular Gift of the Spirit (Irenaeus, *Demonstration of the Apostolic Preaching*, 9). This is the ascent through the stars of which our baptism was the decisive beginning: the Spirit-led journey from earth-centredness, that is, self-centredness, to re-centring in the sun of God's love. Knowing we are loved, then we love him and love others and the earth as he loves them. Not heaven on earth yet, but the beginning of the New Heaven and New Earth.

In some saints, what was experienced powerfully in baptism, but was only the beginning, actually seems to have been completed on earth. The radiant face of the Desert Fathers, monks of the early Christian centuries, 'is a regular feature in the spirituality of the desert', says Daniel Lemeni (Lemeni 2016, p. 49). Abba Arsenius was seen to look like fire (Arsenius 27, in *Give Me a Word*, 2015, p. 45). Abba Sisoes said that he would have become 'all on fire' with just one of the *logismoi* (sayings) of Abba Antony (Sisoes 9, in *Give Me a Word*, p. 283). The shining face, and also the saying of Spirit-inspired words between faces ... Abba Pambo's face was compared with that of Moses shining when he came down from the mountain, and was said to 'shine like lightning, and he was like an emperor sitting on his *throne*' (Pambo 12, in *Give Me a Word*, p. 263, my emphasis). The throne comparison is especially interesting in the light of the transformatory visions of Rabbi Ishmael and other Jewish mystics whose focus was God's throne (*merkabah*). In the nineteenth century, people who met the hermit St Seraphim of Sarov also remembered the blinding light of his face (Varden 2018, p. 128).

If I can add a reminiscence of my own, my godmother had a friend who was a Dominican contemplative nun, Sister Mary Raymund Richmond. Many people, including myself, my family and my confreres, used to write to her asking for prayers, because her gift of intercession was very powerful: some of us nicknamed her 'The Nuclear Option'. I finally got to meet Sr Mary Raymund face to face a year or so into my priestly ministry, which was near the end of her earthly life. By then she was very ill in hospital, and she could take visits of only five minutes. I don't remember anything she said, but I do remember her warm welcome and her joy; and above all the radiance of her face.

This transformation was the fruit of a long struggle not against the body, but against harmful passions that make us addicts because they take away our freedom: not the body broken by ascesis, but even now shining with the resurrection (Lemeni 2016, pp. 51–2).

The image and the mirror

In the ritual of anointing, the face of the new Christians reflects the shining face of God – like a mirror. In this and the previous chapter we saw that Paul uses the image of a mirror:

> For now we see [literally look, *blepomen*] in a mirror, dimly, but then we will see face to face. (1 Cor. 13.12)

> [A]ll of us, with unveiled faces, seeing the glory of the Lord as though reflected in a mirror, are being transformed into the same image from one degree of glory to another. (2 Cor. 3.18)

In the light of these words, we can examine an intriguing passage in the Letter of James (1.22–25). He compares the person who is a hearer of the word but not a doer with someone who considers[4] their 'natural' or 'birth' face in a mirror, then goes away and immediately forgets what they look like. By contrast, 'the one who has bent over towards the law of perfect freedom and has remained, not a hearer becoming forgetful but a doer of work, this one will be blessed in the doing of it' (James 1.25, translated literally). The bending over may be metaphorical, or literal: as Mary Magdalene bent over Jesus' tomb (John 20.11), or Abimelech looked (down?) through the window (Gen. 26.8). Or again, the person who peers through Wisdom's windows (Sir. 14.23). But what is significant in the passage from James is that the person does not just bend over or peer – they remain there. They contemplate. It conjures up images of believers in an Eastern church bent over an icon of Christ or one of the saints, or Roman Catholics bent over in prayer before the exposed Eucharist. And the contemplation is fruitful, becomes 'work', in the relationship with neighbour, seeing God in the other: bridling the tongue, caring for the orphans and widows and keeping oneself 'unstained by the world' (that is, worldly values and the fallen angels that populate the *kosmos*) (James 1.26–27).

Were James's readers contemplating an image? And there is the mystery of the Jordan Lead Codices, initially dismissed when they came to light in 2011, but now shown by metallurgical tests to be at least two hundred years old, and possibly up to two thousand. These small ring-bound lead books contain many images, *including one of a face.*[5]

Patristic commentators tend to reflect on this passage in more metaphorical terms. Oecumenius sees the figure of a mirror as containing examples of moral behaviour (Oecumenius, *Commentary on the Catholic Epistle of James*, 468–469); whereas Bede takes the 'law of freedom' as the grace of the gospel (Bede, *Exposition of the Catholic Epistles*, 17), and Theophylact identifies it with the Law of Christ (Theophylact, *An Accurate Exposition of the Catholic Epistles*, 1148).[28] Nevertheless, since it is also a natural part of the reflection which comes from reading the Word of God or contemplating an image, a symbolic reading is compatible with a more 'concrete' reading of these verses.

If James is indeed talking about the veneration of an image, perhaps of the Risen Lord, then a third term is introduced between self and other. When I see the other, I do not just know that they are made in the image and likeness of God (Gen. 1.26–27) because I heard this read to me in church or read it myself; I *remember* the face of the risen Lord from my prayer before the icon. I have already seen an image of God. Simply by virtue of being human I am always already in relation with the other, as Janet Rayworth said to me, and therefore their face makes an ethical demand on me (Levinas). But on a level of grace the perception is raised higher: through the graced contemplation of an image, I really do see another Christ in the other person, even in one not yet raised up in baptism.

And if the image is really clean, if it is shining in the light, it will also act as a mirror. So in an image of Christ I will literally, physically, see myself. Cleaning of the image (think of those most blessed of volunteers, the church cleaners) is a symbol of purification:

> For you, O God, have tested us; you have tried us as silver is tried. (Ps. 66.10)

> The promises of the LORD are promises that are pure, silver refined in a furnace on the ground, purified seven times. (Ps. 12.6)

Our gaze has to be purified, because we either do not see, or we make idols. Let us turn to a consideration of the image in Christian tradition.

Notes

1 This does not take away from other possible reasons for their anger – such as the 'Son of Man' at the right hand of God being seen as a threat to God's unity (Barrett 1994, pp. 382–5). The pre-existent Son of Man is also seen in the apocryphal 1 Enoch 46—61 (Barrett, pp. 382–5) which, because of its use and influence in the early Church (such as in the Epistle of Jude), might already have generated negative attitudes among non-Christian Jews.

2 I am indebted to Pavlina Marie Kašparova for sharing her expertise in this area.

3 *katanoounti*, from the same verb as 'consider the lilies', Luke 12.27 (see Chapter 4).

4 See www.leadbookcentre.com/jordanian-lead-books.php, and Barker 2017.

5 And see Johnson 1995, pp. 208–9.

6

The Icon: Seeing God, Seeing Our Neighbour

We saw in the last chapter how the use of imagery was highly debated in Judaism. The Commandments forbid 'graven images' (Ex. 20.4–6). Israel longed to see God's face, yet the verses about the Lord shining his face upon you (Num. 6.24–27) could be read but not explained. Moses veiled his shining face, and in a later passage God told him, 'My face you shall not see' (Ex. 33.20).

The emphasis in Deuteronomy is rather on the voice, the word: '*Hear*, O Israel' (Deut. 6.4). Yet early Christian art shows the use of images, including of Christ. While the catacombs are often thought of as the earliest examples, it is difficult to distinguish Christian and pagan symbols there, such as the vine. Indeed, this might have been quite intentional: as Christians were persecuted, they had to hide, which is why they used a secret sign, the fish (see White 2015, p. 26). But in 'safe spaces', behind closed doors, Christians could be free. St James may be referring to an image when he speaks of 'the one who has bent over towards the law of perfect freedom' (James 1.25, my translation), and in the Dura Europus baptistery, we see images of Christ the Good Shepherd, Adam and Eve, and the women at the tomb (see Chapter 5). Images also abound in the fifth- and sixth-century frescoes in the churches of Ravenna, Italy (Figure 6.1[1]). At the same time, there were worries about idol-worship and with religion and politics practically inseparable in the Byzantine Empire, these differences eventually erupted in civil war, the Iconoclastic Controversy (Belting 1994, pp. 144–8). While the Second Council of Nicaea (787) resolved this in favour of the icon (which we will examine below), the problem didn't go away, re-emerging again and again, especially in the Reformations of the sixteenth and seventeenth centuries. Some churches in the Protestant tradition have few or no images to this day – the focus instead, as in Deuteronomy, is on the Word, which flows creatively into music. Perhaps surprisingly, the Catholic Church had its own 'Iconoclast' moment following the reforming Second Vatican Council in the 1960s.

What is this about? First, it's about the second commandment, that we are not to worship the work of our hands. Some Protestant churches observe this very strictly, to the extent of not even having plain crosses. God is, after all, invisible. Images may, then, be too much of a temptation. But the deeper question is what the image says about what we believe. Is it trying to represent what Scripture, the Word of God, teaches us? Or is it no more than a projection? Art always tells the truth about the artist. 'Christian art' is often reproached for being kitsch, such as images of the Holy Spirit that look like a floppy bird. What does such an image say about our faith? The French Dominican priest Marie-Alain Couturier aroused controversy in France in the 1940s and 1950s in rejecting the work of Christian artists and instead commissioning non- (and sometimes anti-) Christian artists such as Picasso, Braque and Matisse to design and decorate churches, on the grounds that their art was alive but much Christian art wasn't (see Lion 2005). Huge amounts of 'traditional' art were thrown out of Catholic churches after the Second Vatican Council on the grounds that it distracted people from focusing on God (too many saints) and/or presented a fixation on repentance and sorrow before a perpetually angry God, forgetting about the Resurrection.

Since then, much has changed. Although Protestant churches tend to major more on lively worship music – the singing of the Word – images are now widely accepted across the Protestant tradition. And with this has come a healthy focus on the *ethics* of the image. Is a particular image of God, of Jesus, a good image in every sense? What does it say about what we believe, our response to the Word of God? And indeed, about our gaze? In Catholicism much of the traditional imagery has returned, but in the context of a more balanced theology.

Yet much Christian art may be seen as illustration, rather than an image for contemplation, for *gazing* at, as in James 1.25. What can theology say about the image? And about the relationship of the image to our gaze on others?

The icon ...

We touched on the icon in Chapter 3, in considering the image(s) of Christ believed to be 'not made with hands' (*acheiropoietos*).[2] We saw their possible origin in the Veronica (the cloth with which a female disciple wiped the face of Christ during his Passion), the face cloth from Jesus' tomb, or the Shroud of Turin. In spite of the extremely confused tradition of legends passed on by what would appear to be a process of Chinese whispers, it may have some basis in fact, even if the images that have come down to us are only copies of copies at best. The tradition suggests that the first Christians valued the image of Christ not because they wanted images to worship, but because God took the initiative in making himself visible in the flesh as Jesus.

St John Damascene, a key theologian for the ending of the iconoclast crisis, argued that the Incarnation of Christ (his taking flesh and thus becoming visible to human beings) permitted human beings to share by grace in the divine status that Christ possessed by nature as Son of God (John Damascene, *Three Treatises*, I.21/p. 35). But John insists, 'I do not depict the invisible divinity [*theotēta*, the divine nature], but I depict God [*theon*, that is, the person of the Son] *made visible in the flesh*' (John Damascene, *Three Treatises*, I.4/p. 22, cited by Mcfarland 2016, p. 162, my emphasis).

This understanding was refined by Theodore the Studite: we cannot depict human nature as such – we must depict *this* person (their hair, eyes and so on). The higher nature of reason, consciousness and will, for example, is invisible. Nor does the image have to be an accurate likeness, as long as it is still recognizable (Theodore the Studite, *On the Holy Icons*, III.A34, C5; Mcfarland 2016, pp. 8–9). And perhaps most importantly, 'in an icon a person is represented "not according to the appearance of his corruptible flesh but according to the glorified body of Christ"' (Mcfarland, p. 169, citing Ouspensky and Lossky 1992, vol. 2, p. 456). So an icon is not an idol. We are seeing Christ or the saint not as he/she would naturally look in this life, nor even as they look in the risen body – which in this life we cannot see – but rather as a *symbol* of the risen body. At his Transfiguration, Christ's body 'became other', translating Luke 9.29 literally. So we see the saints and yet do not see them.

And we can depict saints as well as Christ because, according to Ian Mcfarland, we are images of God through our relationship to the Son, the one image of God – and as the Son is incarnate, he is inseparable from his relationships with human beings. We are in communion with the saints through Christ. And the saints, those who have responded to God's call, remind us that we are called to communion with others. Contemplating the icons of the saints, we are drawn to Christ (see Mcfarland 2016, pp. 169ff.).

In his classic study, *The Art of God Incarnate: Theology and Image in Christian Tradition,* Aidan Nichols says that it is not so much that we look and analyse and decide that this is an image of God, but that we are shown something by God. 'God empowers the "eyes of our mind" with a new "light" so that we can recognize in a visual medium an object which is God himself' (Nichols 1980, p. 137). Of course, we can only see the image of God – as an icon of Christ – *as* God by the light of faith. But

> the eyes of faith can only see when the light of faith falls on them from the divine form of Jesus Christ. The ambiguity is an inbuilt one, just as in looking at pictures a humbling of self before the object is both a condition and an effect of really seeing. (Nichols, pp. 137–8)

In fact, Nichols argues, perception and transformation are vitally interlinked in art. Aesthetic feeling is deep because the aesthetic object reaches into everything that makes us a perceiver of meaning. For example, Henry Moore's *Madonna and Child* can speak to us on the mother/child bond, 'but only on the condition that we *participate* in the artwork through that in us which is capable of being affected by it' (Nichols, p. 138). In other words, we have to be receptive – which is the beginning of love. As Mikel Dufresne says, 'Is not love that expectation of a conversion by the attention we pay to the other, to that which he is and expresses?' (Dufresne 1973, p. 406).

Saints are people who humbly receive the gift of divine love as it is:

> Far from being, then, a pejoratively subjective enthusiasm, emotive, self-indulgent, self-referential, and intellectually dishonest, perception of the form of God in Jesus can only be developed by constant and demanding attention to the image in all its otherness. (Nichols, p. 138)

Contemplation again, remaining there (cf. James 1.25) ... Furthermore,

> the artwork is the taking up of prior materials ... into a new configuration of meaning which the artwork carries as its own immanent significance. It is in its very 'thinghood' the source of power to reinterpret our experience. (p. 139)

According to Philip Sherrard, in the icon its 'holy personages come forth ready to bless and liberate' – converting the beholder from a restricted and limited point of view to the full view of spiritual vision (Sherrard 1962, p. 304). This is because in the icon perspective is inverted, so that rather than our 'seeing into' the picture, the icon sees us (Sigurdson 2016, p. 229) and, as Rowan Williams says, the 'strange skill' of 'reading' an icon is 'letting yourself be seen, be read' (Williams 2000, p. 185).

The icon transforms our fallen world into the heavenly world inhabited by Christ or the saint depicted in the icon. So, as Sigurdson says, it is not so much that we see the icon, but that the icon sees us. Thus the icon also overcomes the connection between the photograph and death seen by Susan Sontag (see Chapter 3): unlike the photograph, which is of the past, an attempt to capture a moment that is hastening towards ageing and death, the icon brings the eternal now of the Resurrection into the here and now.

So the photograph is redeemed: by freezing the moment, it gives us back time to see what we did not have time to see back then, but more, it becomes a sign of the Resurrection in which death will be no more. For the saints share in the divine life, which in the New Heaven and New Earth will reach its fulfilment in the resurrection of the body. And we shall too, if we allow ourselves to be transformed into what we do not know, by letting Christ and his saints see us.

The Presence

Although icons have become more popular in Western Christianity, due in great part to encounters with Russian Orthodox exile communities in Western Europe and the United States following the 1917 Revolution, in Western Catholicism paintings and statues do not have the same status. They are more illustrative, even though they may be, and often are, used for contemplation. But the more common focus for contemplative adoration has been the Eucharist. In the Roman Catholic Church, a long-popular practice has been the adoration of the eucharistic host outside the Mass. The simple reason is that in Catholic teaching the Eucharist really is Christ's body (cf. John 6), and thus he is really present in it. His real presence – *panim*, 'faces'.

Yet this veneration has not been without controversy, even within the Catholic Church: surely Jesus said, 'Take, eat' (Matt. 26.26; cf. John 6.52–58), not 'Look at'? Is there not a risk of idolatry here? Christian communities may seek a 'transignification' approach to the Eucharist: that is, the bread remains bread, but now *signifies* the Body of Christ. For example, R. Berset says:

> The heart of this mystery is that communion with God passes by way of the communion of men [sic] among themselves. It is for this reason that the sign of communion with God is 'the sharing between men', the Eucharist being 'before all else a meal' ('sign of something that, in its turn, is a sign of something else'). (Berset 1976, pp. 166, 176, 179, cited in Marion 1995, p. 265)

The trouble, says Jean-Luc Marion, is that in this model God's presence is limited to the present of the community (these people here and now), and the present of its consciousness. So in fact the community, not God, governs God's eucharistic presence. There is a crucial point here. How many Christian communities, whatever their eucharistic theology, have emphasized the presence of God in the brother or sister, the neighbour, to such an extent that the spiritual becomes evacuated, faith morphs into humanism? We meet real needs, but do not feed our own or one another's spiritual hunger, the desire to see the face of God that Stephen beheld in his vision, so that our faces too might shine. Is there not a danger too that the brother or sister – or the community – becomes an idol? A brother or sister or community, which, for all their goodness, are so fragile and, while mediating God to us, can never be God? And if we are not radiant with the light of God's face, how can we share God's radiance with our brother or sister?

Rather, Marion argues for 'Eucharistic presence ceaselessly provoking the attention of men who fall ecstatically outside of the disposability of the present moment' (Marion 1995, p. 167). This present moment can be thrown away, and is all the more disposable as long as we each remain trapped in our own little world. But we can dare to accept the provocation of the eucharistic presence of Christ and be 'ecstatic', literally to 'stand outside' of our little worlds. The irreducible exteriority of 'the present that Christ makes of himself' prevents idolatry, because Christ's presence maintains *distance*, the distinct separation of persons that enables communion (Marion, p. 169). (We ourselves speak of needing personal space – we fear being swallowed up by the desire of someone who does not see us as we are.) So Christ is really present to us, in the face-to-face, yet not dependent on us for his presence.

So, like the icon that opens forward into our lives in its reverse perspective, the Eucharist overcomes the ephemerality of a communion that is founded on the present time, the present community. The Eucharist is the gift of God, just like the gift of God to Moses of face-to-face presence and word which did not depend on humankind's initiative. The Eucharist makes present to us a future from the past: the Eucharist does not recall Christ's death and Resurrection as if we'd forgotten them – rather 'it relies on an event whose past reality has not disappeared in our day' (Marion, p. 173). It renders this day tenable, 'straining' towards that which is coming to us (Phil. 3.13) – 'until he comes' (1 Cor. 11.26) (p. 173).

But for Marion 'the Eucharist anticipates what we will be, will see, will love: *figura nostra,* the figure of what we will be, but above all ourselves, facing the gift that we cannot yet welcome' (p. 174). The Latin *figura* is '*figure*' in Marion's original French, which includes the meaning of 'face'. The Christian whose face is turned towards the Eucharist has not arrived. The Eucharist does not allow us to become smug. Rather, we gaze, as when gazing at the image of the Risen Lord, at what we are still becoming – now but not yet.

Now but not yet. When exposed for adoration, the Eucharistic host is normally clipped behind a circular window on a stand made of gold- or silver-plate, or brass. The window is surrounded by rays, like the sun (Figure 6.2). The face of Christ, shining like the sun (Rev. 1.18), and us, our faces shining as we pass 'from one degree of glory to another' (2 Cor. 3.18). Yet we do not *see* Christ, nor do we see him gazing at us (remember how the eyes of the Holy Face of Tours are closed; see Chapter 3). Instead of seeing Christ's face, we now see only the appearance of bread. Yet it is bread already transformed into the Body of Christ, anticipating our own transformation: in the eucharistic prayers for the dead, the Roman liturgy prays that God will welcome the dead who have hoped in the Resurrection and 'all who have died in your mercy ... into the light of your face' (Eucharistic Prayer II, Roman Missal, p. 683).

'For seeing you, our God, as you are, we shall be like you for all the ages, and praise you without end' (Eucharistic Prayer III, p. 689).

Here below, faith alone can open us to the presence of God. According to Marion, in the mystical reality *behind*, we are 'summoned to *distance* by the Eucharistic present' (Marion 1995, p. 182, my emphasis). Surely we are summoned to union? But union is only possible if we know God's otherness, if we know that God and I are not identical. If I think God and I are identical, I make an idol of myself. The miracle of divinization is that the human being, the image of God that is nevertheless not God, is taken up in God and, having rejected all that is not God, becomes at last him- or herself and receives all things, like St Benedict (see p. 115 below).

It does require conversion: '[T]he one who prays undertakes to let his [sic] gaze be converted in it – thus, in addition, to modify his thought in it' (Marion, p. 182). What this comes down to is the priority of prayer so that we may win in the 'struggle between human impotence to receive and the insistent humility of God to fulfil' (p. 182). Contemplating Christ, like the newly baptized in the early Church who shone with anointing but were not yet fully sanctified, we too are 'now but not yet'. The eucharistic 'now', Christ's presence, exposes our need for grace, our 'not yet'.

And the other person

We live at a time when relationships seem so fragile, when the idea of marriage 'till death do us part' is seen by many as unrealistic or even undesirable.

So in the light of the contemplation of the icon or of the Eucharist, how can we, or how do we, see our fellow human beings? Can we apply what was said above to seeing the face of the other person? For example, Aidan Nichols's words about the icon: 'God empowers the "eyes of our mind" with a new "light" so that we can recognize in a visual medium an object which is God himself' (Nichols 1980, p. 137)? As Christians, we are empowered by the light of faith to see the image and likeness of God in the other person. Following Nichols's argument, does not looking at the face of the other person require 'a humbling of self before the object' (that is, the person) as 'both a condition and an effect of really seeing' (p. 138). And there are Mikel Dufresne's words, 'Is not love that expectation of a conversion by the attention we pay to the other, to which he is and expresses?' (Dufresne 1973, p. 406). Likewise, to see the other person, 'perception of the form of God in Jesus', and, let us add, in all people, 'can only be developed by constant and demanding attention to the image *in all its otherness*' (Nichols 1980, p. 138, my emphasis). Contemplating my neighbour.

Are the icon and my neighbour interchangeable, then? What if they are doing something objectively wrong, which we Christians would call sin? If they reject God? If they reject love? If, on the bus, British George is gazing hatefully at Magda speaking on her phone in her native Polish? Shouting insults at her?

We cannot say that what is patently not of God in the other is reflecting the image of God. The icon, after all, is a symbol of the someone – Christ or a saint – in the perfection of risen glory. The Eucharist we adore, the sacramental Body of Christ, both shows and conceals the perfect image of God that we are becoming but cannot yet see. The other person is made in God's image, yet is also subject, like me, to the Fall, and it would be uncharitable to them for me not to recognize that – quite apart from making an idol out of them. Yet how do I recognize this without judging the other person?

Ian Mcfarland, whom we quoted above, is concerned with what it means to see someone, and how icons may enable us to do this. So he observes that icons are never in profile but full or three-quarter face. And though the artist is anonymous, the icon is not complete until it is named:

> These two ideas – that seeing a person involves looking them in the *face* and acknowledging that a face belongs to a particular *someone* – point to the anthropological significance of icons as liturgical primers for interpersonal encounters in the here and now. (Mcfarland 2016, p. 158)

Christ makes us persons, 'some*ones* as well as some*things*' (Mcfarland, p. 164). This is why saints, responding to God's call, remind us that we are summoned to communion with others. Mcfarland sees central value in the icon's presentation of a body. While critical of a tendency in icon spirituality to treat it as a ladder to the invisible, leaving the embodied behind, he also says that just because we can't encounter a person apart from their body, it 'does not follow that a person is reducible to his or her body, for a body changes over time in ways that can – and generally do – include the loss or destruction of parts' (p. 168) – for example, baldness, mental deterioration, or amputation. Icons, he says, 'stop us reducing people to bodies and at the same time seeing them apart from body'. Icons of saints teach us to see persons. So perhaps the primary pedagogy in icons is teaching us not to mentally disembody (Mcfarland thinks we do this because bodies die), yet to contemplate the other person in order to see the 'more' that is there. Hopefully this graced perspective will prevent us from either judging the other by their body, or lusting after their body – in both cases, failing to see the person. Instead we die to the image we project on them and rise to the person who presents, indeed reveals, themselves to us – or may be happier to do so if we are more receptive. So while I am rightly appalled by the hostility of native British George to Polish Magda on the bus, maybe I should also see the hurt in George. Perhaps, after leaving a failing school with few qualifications, he has struggled to find work in a town with few employment opportunities, and is struggling to survive in the face of benefit cuts; while Magda arrived in his town from Warsaw with a Master's degree and fluent English, took the cleaning job she didn't consider beneath her, and now has her own cleaning company. If I am prepared to see more, I can see the sin of the world behind the personal sin, and far from excusing the personal sin, it might motivate me as a Christian to ask God what he wants me to do about healing the situation.

Pope Francis expresses special concern for what the gaze means for relationships, opposing the loving gaze to the ephemeral, and seeing our gaze on the other person in contemplative terms:

> Loving another person involves the joy of contemplating and appreciating their innate beauty and sacredness, which is greater than my needs. This enables me to seek their good even when they cannot belong to me, or when they are no longer physically appealing but intrusive and annoying. For 'the love by which one person is pleasing to another depends on his or her giving something freely' (Thomas Aquinas, *Summa Theologiae*, 1a2ae.110.1 resp, paraphrased). The aesthetic experience of love is expressed in that 'gaze' which contemplates other persons as ends in themselves, even if they are infirm, elderly or physically unattractive. A look of appreciation has enormous importance, and to begrudge it is usually hurtful. How many things do spouses and children sometimes do in order to be noticed! Much hurt and many problems result when we stop looking at one another. This lies behind the complaints and grievances we often hear in families: 'My husband does not look at me; he acts as if I were invisible'. 'Please look at me when I am talking to you!' 'My wife no longer looks at me, she only has eyes for our children'. 'In my own home nobody cares about me; they do not even see me; it is as if I did not exist'. Love opens our eyes and enables us to see, beyond all else, the great worth of a human being. The joy of this contemplative love needs to be cultivated. (Pope Francis, *Amoris Laetitia* (AL) 127–129)

The combination of gazes and words, of 'faces' and 'sayings', is poignant. Words of hurt and a sense of abandonment come from an experience of non-gaze, of not being seen. But a Christian gaze connects the Holy Trinity of one God, Father, Son and Holy Spirit, with human families: 'we have contemplated the relationship ... [w]ith a gaze of faith and love, grace and fidelity' (AL 29). Jesus' loving gaze accompanies us (AL 60). Pope Francis then encourages couples preparing for marriage to direct their gaze to the future (AL 218), in a way that somewhat recalls Marion on the future orientation of eucharistic presence. It is a gaze towards the future that is about seeing reality: not expecting the other to be perfect, or expecting them to be God for us, but rather gazing together on a 'third' reality (think of Agnès and JR looking out on the lake together at the end of *Faces Places,* see Chapter 3). Yet where people participate in the Church's life 'in an incomplete manner', sometimes because of messy marriage situations, Pope Francis insists that the Church's loving gaze turns towards them and recognition of the work of divine grace in their lives is illumined by the gaze of Jesus Christ. So the gaze of Christ informs the Church's teaching, gazing on the other.

And it flows back. Francis insists:

> It is a profound spiritual experience to contemplate our loved ones with the eyes of God and to see Christ in them. This demands a freedom and openness which enable us to appreciate their dignity. We can be fully present to others only by giving fully of ourselves and forgetting all else. Our loved ones merit our complete attention. Jesus is our model in this, for whenever people approached to speak with him, he would meet their gaze, directly and lovingly (cf. Mark 10.21). No one felt overlooked in his presence, since his words and gestures conveyed the question: 'What do you want me to do for you?' (Mark 10.51) ... We are constantly reminded that each of those who live with us merits complete attention, since he or she possesses infinite dignity as an object of the Father's immense love. This gives rise to a tenderness which can 'stir in the other the joy of being loved'. (AL 323)

We do not contemplate Jesus in the other and in that way find them bearable, failing to see the person. Instead, we need to give that person full attention as Jesus did, because that person is an object of the Father's love. The fruit: the joy of being loved – which has come from being seen. This is the unfolding of something that starts as basic as a 'kind look' (AL 100) – not a forced smile, but a fruit of contemplating Christ's gaze on us. The Pope also encourages appreciating the beauty of another – beauty is not seen as primarily a temptation, but rather 'that "great worth" which is other than physical or psychological appeal', and that 'enables us to appreciate the sacredness of a person, *without feeling the need to possess it*' (AL 127, my emphasis).

So our gaze is both passive/receptive to the other person and to God's image in them – and actively our gaze glorifies them. As Ola Sigurdson says, the gaze on God and the gaze on the other person come together in the celebration of the liturgy: public and private prayer and mutual dependence. No empty rite, but constituting the faith of believer, making an icon of the world, teaching us to see the world as God sees it (like Rabbi Ishmael's experience, Chapter 4): 'Through the liturgy the believer experiences the world as God's world ... The gaze for the invisible is namely not given outside of a *fellowship* that cultivates ... the liturgical gaze' (Sigurdson 2016, pp. 275, 291 – my emphasis).

This includes the person we are gazing on in the Sign of Peace, and flows out to our daily lives. We receive our neighbour because God receives us. And part of the humility of our gaze is that, just as the icon is 'other', representing our transfigured state, which we need to receive in a state of unknowing, so the other person is also other. There is always more to see. The difference is that the icon represents a fundamental transformation to a new kind of existence. But as God receives us with love, so we gaze with love on the other, and it is love that transforms, in God's good time, for eternity. Jean-Luc Marion observes:

> Too much to see there, too much to envisage and look at squarely, too much to interpret and to allow to interpret us, 'and so it flees'. Only Love, bearing all, can bear with its gaze Love's excess. Our gaze can open, even if only by blinking, to the evidence of Love. In this proportion also, bedazzlements can become evidence. (Marion 2002, p. 67; cf. Horner 2005, pp. 66–71)

The bedazzlement of the adored Eucharist? Of the icon, symbol of the Resurrection?

But there is still a problem which can make the Christian gaze (as we might call it) difficult in practice. Yes, in theory I receive the other person as they are, all well and good. But, in practice, does my image of the 'image and likeness of God' get in the way? Do I really see Magda and George, Jean-Luc,

Aidan and Francis? Do I really love them, or just care for them impersonally as my 'neighbour' (so much safer than getting involved, letting the other disturb me)? On the other hand, is there not an opposite risk that – again with all the best intentions – I get so involved with the neighbour/brother/sister as image and likeness of God that I demand that the other *be* God? That I forget the gaze of God *qua* God in Jesus Christ, enabling my necessarily imperfect self to love my necessarily imperfect neighbour?

How to hold this tension, not to tip to one side or the other? Do we need a third term, something that connects love of God and love of neighbour?

The vision of God: Nicholas of Cusa

Perhaps the most original Christian response ever to the question of the gaze is that of the early Renaissance thinker and bishop Nicholas of Cusa (1401–64). To help the Benedictine monks of Tegernsee, Bavaria, to resolve their differences with some Carthusian monks over the significance of non-knowing for contemplative prayer, a debate which had become heated, Nicholas sent them a treatise entitled *On the Vision of God* (VG). To this treatise he attached an image. He calls the image an 'icon' – whether it was an icon made according to the canons of Eastern Christian art, or a Western image, we don't know (Falque 2014; Marion 2016), because it is now lost. It may have been an image believed to be based on the 'not made with human hands' Veronica or Shroud (see Chapter 3). Effectively, the icon and treatise together were a work of multimedia art (Albertson 2019, pp. 262–3; Nicholas of Cusa, VG, p. 324 n. 13).

What we do know is what Nicholas tells us in the preface of the treatise: this image of the face of Christ was 'omnivoyant' – 'seeing everything'. Hence wherever you stood, Christ seemed to be looking at you. (So different from the 'Holy Face of Tours', whose eyes are closed.) So Nicholas instructs the monk reading the text ('you' singular), that before the community starts reading the treatise, he should put the image up on a wall. Wherever you stand, he says to the monk, you'll see that Christ is looking at you. Cross the room, and you'll see his gaze follows you.

Next – find another brother. Brother A stands on one side of the room, Brother B on the other. Both can see the icon. Then, Brother A and Brother B walk forward till they reach the opposite side of the room, crossing each other. And of course both monks, simultaneously, see Christ looking at them, even though, as they move, they are in an infinite number of different places: though also, when they cross, they are at that moment in the same place. And finally, when they reach the opposite sides of the room, they are standing in each other's places. Empathy through image and choreography ...

Of course, to find out what Brother A has seen, Brother B needs to speak to Brother A, and vice versa (de Certeau 1987, p. 27). Not just seeing the face of the other (and this third – or first? – face of Christ), but saying that they have (Levinas). And when they speak, they will find out that they have seen the same thing. And that they have been seen. Seeing the other, who has seen the same as me, even though he is a different person – so how can our discussions with one another become heated? And it was not that we saw first, but that God saw us ... How fitting for resolving a dispute about not knowing God.

This too is not just philosophical, but also profoundly biblical. Nicholas's work is not just a take on all the experiments on perspective and mirrors that artists were carrying out at the time (de Certeau, p. 18), though this must have been an inspiration. But here in Nicholas of Cusa is the whole tradition of Exodus, seeing the face of God and being transformed by the face of God as if it were a mirror; *and* the Deuteronomic tradition of hearing the voice. Seeing and speaking. Nicholas almost seems to anticipate the far more damaging and long-lasting dispute between Protestants (the Word) and Catholics (the image)...

Nicholas's choreography is also essentially Trinitarian – the triangle between the icon, Brother A and Brother B: each seeing the icon seeing them, each seeing each other see the icon seeing them, and talking about it (Logos, Word ...). Far removed from the images of the Trinity often found in eighteenth-century English churches: a triangle with a single, staring eye in the middle of it: the single eye of the Cyclops; or the security camera (or indeed the laptop camera); the modern version of Foucault's surveillance society (see Chapter 2); or again, the terrible eye in the plug-hole after Marion's murder in Alfred Hitchcock's film *Psycho* ... And now the bodily aesthetics ruled by the mobile phone camera (see Chapter 1). Instead, the multiple yet united Trinitarian gaze, of God who is a communion of love. The therapeutic 'miracle of the third':[3] beyond the either/or conflictual dualism of Satan (whose name means 'accuser' or 'opposer'), mirrored in the dispute of the monks whose debate has produced more heat than light.

All this, and they haven't yet read a single word of the treatise.

When they do, they find that Nicholas delights in 'coincidence' – a unity which is manifested in apparent opposites, contradictories. They're found in nature, such as the tree and the seed – each is in the other (VG 22.99). They're found in God himself – God is absolutely simple, yet he is Father, Son and Holy Spirit. God *is*, yet he does all. His seeing, loving and being are all one (wherever you stand, you see his seeing you, loving you, VG 4/10). His moving and resting are the same (VG 9). God sees each person and thing individually and all at the same time (VG 10). He embraces otherness in unity, as Jesus is fully God and fully human, the infinity of God embracing and taking up the finitude of human nature. This is dizzying, it is a seeing 'beyond the wall of Paradise' as Nicholas often says, a seeing that is not seeing yet rests in a deeper truth that overcomes our oppositions, and instead grasps the incomprehensible and says what cannot be said.

Daringly, Nicholas says that God is called *Theos* in Greek because he sees (*theorein*) (VG 1). Nicholas's learned monks would probably have known Greek, and would have known the contemplative seeing, the mutual seeing, of Mary Magdalene (John 21.18), and those who gaze on the Son and so will have eternal life (John 6.40) (see Chapter 4). We can argue about Nicholas's etymologies – but, like St Anselm's argument that

God must exist because nothing greater than God can be thought, or Karl Barth's insistence on God being beyond all philosophical arguments for his existence and our not questioning God but God questioning us, we might not be convinced by the argument but the question that comes from it won't let us go. We don't know yet we know; we know yet we don't know. To borrow a Cusan phrase, we're in a state of 'learned ignorance'.

We could, of course, say that the whole thing is a giant optical illusion. We don't see God, we see a picture which *seems* to see you (and anyone else) wherever they're standing. So Nicholas insists (VG 6) that we see the face of God not with eyes of flesh but eyes of the mind and intellect. There's no quantity or quality in God's face (such as colour) – rather, God's face is the truth, preceding every formable face, exemplar of all faces. 'Every face, therefore, which can behold your face sees nothing that is other or different from itself, because it sees there its own truth' (6/18). So if we look lovingly, we see loving faces, look angrily, see angry faces. This is not, to take the early example, to deny the hatefulness of George's gaze on Magda: but it is to see that there is more to George than his hatred. Again, we are close to Levinas – seeing the face of the other – and Nicholas has taken us in a stroke from the intellectual contemplation of God beyond the senses to the God-informed seeing the other person with my eyes – this person who sees me. The evacuation of all concepts of God enables us to do what we have to do to see another – to evacuate all prior concepts of that person. Ethics before ontology ... Thus, says Nicholas, 'In all faces the face of faces is seen veiled and in enigma' (VG 21, cf. 1 Cor. 13.12). It is not seen until we enter into a 'certain secret and hidden silence beyond all faces where there is no knowledge or concept of a face' – into cloud, mist, ignorance – then it is revealed, like the sun veiled in stars and in the colours of things. In a leap we must go beyond visible light. We leap into the darkness, then see God in the face of the other and in the entire creation – God, says Nicholas, is in fact completely visible (VG 12). We think we look in a mirror, yet we are the mirror, God is the one seeing ...

And the holier we become, the truer mirror of God we will be. Nicholas, almost imperceptibly amid his high-wire performance of opposites, has shifted in VG 6 to addressing God, and now, in a style very reminiscent of late medieval *Devotio Moderna*, 'modern devotion', addresses Jesus:

> And more subtly still, from a few signs you comprehended what lay hidden in the mind of a human being. For nothing is conceived in the mind that is not in some way signalled in the face, most greatly in the eyes, because the face is the heart's messenger. (VG 22/94)

From one sign he got the concept of whole person – like the learned who can describe the author's whole purpose from just glancing at a book. Jesus grasped all from every gesture of the eyes as a deaf person does from movement of another's lips.

And Jesus' being, seeing and loving are one and the same, because he is God. United with us, he unites us with God, and we will see others as God sees them, revealing God to them and them to themselves.

Like Ola Sigurdson, Catherine Pickstock is concerned with gaze in the liturgy, in which she finds the Cusan coincidence of opposites. For example, in the Roman Rite of Mass (both pre-Vatican II, which Pickstock analyses, and modern) the priest says to the people, 'May the peace of the Lord be with you always'. But after the peace, we pray that the Lamb of God may grant us peace. As Pickstock says, the request for peace can only be made from within peace, but 'its attainment is not a static arrival at, but a perpetual asking for peace' (Pickstock 1998, p. 238). We receive the gift only by giving back (p. 240) – like Brother A and Brother B who both give to and receive from each other the knowledge of what they have seen, even though they have seen Christ looking at them at opposite ends of the room – a paradox, an impossibility. And as Pickstock says regarding peace, we are never outside God, as worshippers, yet have fallen away from God (pp. 229–30). Arguably we are in liturgical time, a liturgical space – an in-between, a divine middle (see Chapter 4) which is also a communion. We have to keep asking, keep praying without ceasing to see God and to see our neighbour.

And for all the influence of the visual experiments of Nicholas's artist contemporaries, Johannes Hoff believes that his approach is essentially liturgical:

> As distinct from this new tradition, Cusa's *vera icona* did not have the character of art image in which the viewer is expected to immerse him or herself. Rather it was designed to serve as a liturgical image that can be approached simultaneously from a plurality of viewpoints like a sacramental threshold that mediates between the earthly liturgical gathering of the church and the fullness of the divine glory without blurring the difference between the human and the divine. In short, Cusa's icon was designed to recover the pre-modern, *liturgical* concept of space. (Hoff 2013, p. 55)

There are many paradoxes in the liturgy. In the Roman Rite in its pre-Vatican II form (the so-called Extraordinary Form), along with many Eastern Rite and older Anglican/Reformed liturgies, the priest faces the altar, or 'back to the people'. God told Moses in Exodus 33.44 that he would only see God's back, because he could not see God's face and live, a prophecy perhaps not fulfilled in Moses' lifetime (see Chapter 4). When the priest turns to the people and shows the Eucharist, he says, 'Behold the Lamb of God'. The people see the Eucharist, bread and wine transformed into the Body and Blood of Christ: his real presence, the Bread of Heaven. The people do not see Christ's face. They see *a* face, but that is the face of the priest, 'in the person of Christ the head' according to Catholic teaching (*Catechism of the Catholic Church*, 1548). In the modern Roman and many Anglican rites, the priest faces the people for all of the Mass – seeing the face of God. Again, this is not *actually* the face of God – yet it somehow represents it. A popular Catholic devotion is adoration of the Eucharist outside of Mass: the consecrated host is enclosed in a monstrance, literally, 'a showing device'. Most commonly this is a stand with the host enclosed behind a circular glass, with a frame of golden rays – the blazing sun of Christ's face at his Transfiguration or when John saw him in Revelation (Rev. 1.16). Yet we see no face. Liturgy, the time of between, of middle – now and not yet. In the same way as the other is the image of God, and yet not God – so at the same time the other is not just Brother A or Brother B, but the image of God: the image of God who is and sees and loves us. And a God whose gaze surprises us: one moment in the image, next in the liturgy and in the face of the priest, then in the faces of George and Magda, so that I always need to pray to see God and see the person before me.

We might, then, become quite good at gazing, our gaze holy because it is a graced response to God's gaze. A gaze that really sees and loves that person, delights in finding out more about them, whether or not, as Pope Francis points out, they are actually attractive to us.

But we are erotic beings. We desire. Not only did Plato recognize this in the *Symposium* (see Chapter 4), but God himself put desire in Adam and Eve – how else would they 'increase and multiply' (Gen. 1.28)? What then of the erotic gaze? Is there not a risk that a Christian theology of the gaze will see only the sin in the hypersexualized gaze that dominates social media? Is there nothing good to be said of desire for another person, for the erotic gaze?

Notes

1 All images are available to view online at: https://scmpress.hymnsam.co.uk/media/74923/images-for-how-do-i-look.pdf.

2 Note also the tradition that Saint Luke painted the Blessed Virgin Mary (Schaefer 1986).

3 Carl Jung was interested in Nicholas of Cusa for the psychological significance of the coincidence of opposites, and the therapist as the person in the dangerous position of being committed to 'this as well as that' (Henderson 2010, p. 102, citing Jung 1969, p. 679). However, Jung's own inexorable drive for the quaternity leads him to be somewhat dismissive of the Trinity as dependent on an earlier stage of humankind's spiritual development (Jung 1970).

7

Erotic Gaze, Celibate Gaze: Theotic Gaze

The theology that has grown through the icon in the Christian East and the gaze on the Eucharist in Western Catholicism has provided resources for the Church to gaze on the God we cannot see and to gaze lovingly in God on our brother and sister whom we can see (cf. 1 John 4.20). But 2,000 years of history reveal a catalogue of sins of the gaze. On one level, this is obvious: Christians are sinners; we don't automatically stop sinning after baptism (see Romans 6—7). Indeed, we would not need to discuss the subject of the gaze if it were natural to us to gaze lovingly at others.

But there has been a specific problem around the gaze in 2,000 years of the Church, and that has been around the issue of desire. The erotic gaze ... Most recently there has been the horrific revelation of sexual abuse of children and vulnerable adults by clergy and members of religious communities. Victims are still coming forward and there is a lot of repentance and healing still to take place. Among many other issues, hard questions need to be asked about formation in chastity.

Too often we did not bring the issue of chastity into God's gaze; we did not let God see the most intimate place of our desire. There has, nevertheless, been good work done on spiritual and psychological integration. But a fundamental question the Church has always been working with – and which affects people in every vocation and walk of life – is what Jesus meant by looking lustfully at a woman (Matt. 5.27–28).

In the early Christian centuries, a major influence on Christian thought on this and many other questions was Platonist philosophy. This was not just because it was the dominant philosophy in the culture of the time, just as this book has engaged with contemporary secular thinkers. Rather, Platonism was especially attractive because not only did it insist on the existence of a heavenly world, but the world of ideals and forms (which are imperfectly realized in the 'particulars' of the physical world) fitted in very well with God asking Moses to model the Tabernacle on the vision he had on Mount Sinai – and Jesus obtaining 'a more perfect liturgy' from heaven (Heb. 8.6; see White 2019). We saw from the *Symposium*, examined in Chapter 4, a powerful philosophy of ascent through desire to the vision of a wondrous beauty. Each state of the ascent is a higher love. It starts with physical desire for the body of another – in this case, in fact, the desire of older men for the bodies of teenage boys. In the ambient culture of Ancient Greece, this was manifested in sexual acts and could not be described as consensual. The best the young man might hope for was a certain patronage, including education (see Dover 1978, pp. 81–110, 202–3).

Nowadays – at last – such behaviour, which has also manifested in the Church, is rightly treated as abuse and a criminal offence. At least in Plato's ascent it was left behind, but it clearly offered no model for human sexuality that would be compatible with the teachings of Jesus. Furthermore, the leaving behind of sexual love in Plato could mean, and often did mean, that the physical was treated with disdain by Christian theologians who made positive use of Plato's philosophy of ascent. As Denise Carmody has pointed out, 'the fears of matter, the body, the flesh' in early Christianity worked 'to the special disadvantage of women', as bleeding and giving birth tended to mark women as unclean (Carmody 1995, p. 135). And of course if men looked at women and were physically attracted to them, this could become a problem for their chastity – for which women were often blamed for being attractive or just visible. According to this view, it was not that the man sinned by looking, but that the woman's looks provoked and seduced him. Uta Ranke-Heinemann (1990, pp. 35ff.) has put together a catalogue of appalling male clergy attitudes towards women.

St John Chrysostom (*c.* 349–407) regards women as a temptation to priests (*On the Priesthood* VI.8). Predictably these slurs were accompanied by injunctions about how women must cover up and not look at men (see, for example, Clement of Alexandria, *Christ the Educator*, II.110–117; Ambrose, *On Penance*, I.14.14). All Eve's fault, in other words. According to Possidius' *Life of Augustine* (26/pp. 225–6), the great bishop, philosopher and theologian allowed no unaccompanied woman into his home. And as late as the 1890s, in a church in which priestly celibacy was obligatory, Pope St John XXIII wrote in his journal as a young seminarian that he must have no familiar relationships with women, must be cautious even with relatives, and devout women (Roncalli 1980, p. 7). It is only in the post-Conciliar period that women have started to take senior positions (and indeed positions at all) in the Vatican government and university institutions of the Catholic Church in Rome.

This is so far removed, as Ranke-Heinemann points out, from Jesus' easy friendships with women (1990, p. 102). And is indeed oblivious of a far from obscure part of the Bible – Genesis 1.27: 'So God created humankind in his image, in the image of God he created them; male and female he created them'. Yet it had reached a point where women were being treated by senior clergy as if they were not only invisible, but non-existent.

For Ranke-Heinemann, this is both cause and effect of a Church that is implacably hostile to the body and sexuality. Admittedly, the objectivity of her analysis has been seriously questioned (Shortt 2019): to take just one example, Augustine actually says in his Rule that it is no sin for the celibate brothers of his community to look at women (see below). Also, just as Christians today operate in cultural contexts with which we unthinkingly or knowingly compromise (what will future generations think about early twenty-first-century Christian behaviour in the face of climate change, poverty, beginning- and end-of-life vulnerability, exclusion ...?), so Christians like Clement and Augustine lived in cultures where gender segregation and the control of women was a social norm. There may even have been fear of Christian freedom leading to scandal or false allegations. Even up to the 1970s in rural Italy, a young couple could not go out for the day together without the girl phoning home hourly (Rist 2005, p. 85).

But that is no excuse. Massive damage has been done to the dignity and authority of women in the Church, and to the Church as a whole. And one might ask whether the terrible abuse of minors and vulnerable adults which has come to light in the Catholic Church would have carried on for so long and to such an extent if more women had been in positions of governance.

For all that, it is possible to find different voices in the tradition. And this is urgent at a time when, as we saw at the beginning of this book, body image has become a mental health problem in our society. Not only is society hypersexualized, with virginity being treated as a stigma and even grounds for 'undateability' (Hunt 2019), but bodies become 'successful' or 'unsuccessful', as Regina Ammicht-Quinn has said (see Chapter 1), and they can be enhanced, but a weak male body or a fat female body become cause for shame. 'Saying no' is no longer about sex, but about food (Ammicht-Quinn 2009, pp. 72–4). In the light of that, could Christian teaching on chastity, and even the particular vocation of celibacy, be able to offer a gaze that loves rather than rates the other person? But we must not circumvent the question of the erotic gaze, neutralizing it or 'making up' for it with celibacy. As we recalled at the end of the last chapter, God himself put desire in Adam and Eve – how else would they 'increase and multiply' (Gen. 1.28)?

This points to the need for a Christian theology of eros. In early 1962, just when traditional European norms about the role of women, the body and sexuality were starting to be questioned, Pope St John XXIII, the once demure seminarian who sought to avert his gaze from women, is remembered as opening his arms wide on meeting America's First Lady, Jacqueline Kennedy, and calling her by her first name (McAuley 2015). Two years earlier a young Polish theologian, Karol Wojtyła, the future Pope St John Paul II, published *Love and Responsibility*, which marked the beginnings of what is now called

'Theology of the Body'. Drawing on his experience of pastoral work with married couples, he recognizes that Church rules of so-called sexual morality 'often run up against greater difficulties in practice than in theory' (Wojtyła 1981 [1960], p. 16). So he decides to change the approach completely. He shifts the focus from rules to the person, and from use to love. Drawing on Personalist philosophy as well as Scripture, Wojtyła understands human beings as persons, somebodies rather than somethings (cf. Mcfarland 2016; see Chapter 6), who are both subject and object, and capable of love. The biblical commandment to love is the greatest. So in terms both of philosophy and revelation humankind must put love first. It is the context for our sexuality, and in Genesis, as we have seen, human sexuality is procreative and as such a participation in God's creative work. For Wojtyła, our God-given rational nature is a natural help in using our sexuality responsibly, not just acting on instinct. One cannot use the other person – Wojtyła acknowledges a truth in the pessimism of the rigorists – but a couple can share joy in their sexuality through mutual understanding and collaboration. Not the most romantic language, perhaps, but his basis is relationality and loving the other, from which shared joy can come.

This also means that Wojtyła sees no moral problem with attraction. He gives what amounts almost to a history of a relationship. Desire arises most basically in acknowledgement of our limitations and our need for other beings. Being a man or a woman also means that a man is not a woman, a woman is not a man: that is a limitation. Hence the sense of 'You are good for me' (Wojtyła, p. 82). Of course, that is self-centred. For my love to be real, it must grow into love for your good. There is no love if the two parties are just using each other. And the emotion of sympathy alone is too weak. Friendship is needed, willing good for you as I desire it for myself (p. 90).

The implications for the gaze are enormous. Not only does Wojtyła's theology exclude any Christian view of marriage as simply a means of continuing the human race, but his insistence on friendship in marriage requires that two people really see the other, and indeed hear the other: how else can one partner begin to understand what really is the good of the other partner?

And friendship (both in marriage and out of it) cannot last unless there is equality. If I regard the other person as not equal to me in dignity, either I am contemptuous or condescending, or else – if I think them superior – I am putting them on a pedestal and not loving the real person in their inevitable fragility. The problem – and this is in no ways confined to Christianity – is that we tend to treat 'equal' as meaning 'the same'. As soon as we encounter difference, we want to order it into a hierarchy of superior or inferior (cf. Deleuze and Guattari 1987, p. 9). Everything has to be reduced to one in a vertical hierarchy. Whereas God created humankind as equal *and different* from the beginning, male and female reflecting what would later emerge in Christian revelation as the unity-in-difference that is the Trinity. This enables us not just to appreciate equality in gender difference, but also the equality that is present when two or more people are present.

So chastity, for Wojtyła, must not just be a rule that we resent. It must be integrated into the person, as part of love for the other person, rather than using the other, however unconsciously, for my own gratification (Wojtyła, pp. 145–7). Emotional attraction can put a natural brake on this – although, Wojtyła reminds us, that can also arise from a need to be 'in love' or to feel loved, and in fact only places a lyrical mask over a basically sexual desire for the other person.

Is he making unrealistic demands? Wojtyła is quick to point out 'a spontaneous sensual reaction' – being physically and/or emotionally attracted to someone – is no sin (p. 162). Rather, what matters is what our will then does with a perfectly normal and natural experience. Do I just indulge myself, pretending to love the other person – or do I see the integration that turns the natural attraction into a loving interaction with the other as that person? Chastity, Wojtyła argues, belongs to love, and is there to govern all tendencies to use others, wherever these tendencies arise from. And because it frees physical and emotional desire, and even marriage, from association with lust and using the other, chastity actually frees us from disdain for sex and the body and disparagement of marriage. Such prudish attitudes are, Wojtyła believes, the fruit of unchastity – whereas real chastity is manifested *in the gaze*: 'To be chaste means to have a "transparent" attitude to a person of the other sex' (p. 170; he is obviously speaking of heterosexual attraction, but this does not take away from the universal application of his principle of transparency).

What about the gaze and shame? We saw in Chapter 2 how Lacan noted our shame when we realize that our gaze on the other is being observed. Wojtyła takes a similar approach – shame is the fear that what a person believes should remain hidden in them may come out into the open (p. 175). But he takes it further, acknowledging the work of anthropologists which has demonstrated that nudity as such is, universally speaking, neither a matter of modesty or immodesty, given its cultural variability (think of the nudity involved in the early Christian baptismal liturgies, Chapter 5). Wojtyła shows that the widespread instinct for self-covering or visual distance springs from a desire to be really loved and not used. You must not touch me, even in your thoughts. (Of course – Wojtyła does not cover this – an overwhelming desire to be loved can override this instinct; so great is our desire that I project on to the other person the belief that they really love me unconditionally. Or I think that at least an intimate encounter with them, even if it's ephemeral, will make me feel better. Using the other and allowing ourselves to be used: after the Fall, God says to Eve, 'Your desire shall be for your husband, and he shall rule over you' (Gen. 3.16). The perfect analysis of the abusive relationship.)

By contrast, the desire of a couple making love not to be seen by others stems, at its deepest level, from the fact that they know that only they know their love, and they need to be safe, trustingly, to lose control and become one in flesh (cf. Gen. 2.24): 'shame (at being seen) is ... swallowed up by love' (Wojtyła, pp. 181, 182).

In terms of our gaze, although 'shame is a tendency, uniquely characteristic of the human person, to conceal sexual values sufficiently to prevent them from obscuring the value of person as such', prudery 'consists in regard to concealing one's real intentions', pretending to have no physical/sexual interests because of a belief that such things are wrong (pp. 187, 188). Clearly such an attitude betokens neurosis, a state of being at war with oneself. Of course, modesty in behaviour and dress is important: we know that there are ways of behaving and dressing that are very likely to provoke a lustful gaze or action towards us. We have to be realistic.

But we are not required to be slaves of the unchastity of others. Conversion of the gaze is what is needed. And clearly what amounts to modesty varies between contexts (e.g. street versus swimming pool). But we can also dress in a way that attracts love and nurtures situations for loving encounters. In that respect the attitudes of the early Fathers manifest immaturity. In the past hundred years men and women have learnt to be friends and are learning to be equals. Platonic friendships between men and women are one of the jewels of our age, and may or may not lead to marriage. In this respect Wojtyła was prophetic in insisting that friendship is integral to marriage. This requires an ability to gaze chastely, that is, lovingly, on the other person.

We saw in Chapter 3 the power of visual art to depict not just the subject (e.g. a human being) but the gaze on that person. Wojtyła insists that, on the grounds of beauty,

> art has a right and a duty, for the sake of realism, to reproduce the human body, and the love of man and woman, as they are in reality, to speak the whole truth about them. The human body is an authentic part of the truth about man, just as its sensual and sexual aspects are an authentic part of the truth about human love. But it would be wrong to let this part obscure the whole – and this is what often happens in art. (p. 192)

But pornography obscures rather than reveals. It is not a true gaze. Whereas

> there are circumstances in which nakedness is not immodest. If someone takes advantage of such an occasion to treat the persona as an object of enjoyment ... it is only he who is guilty of shamelessness ... not the other. (Wojtyła, p. 190)

Hence the image in Christian art of nude human beings in their natural state in heaven, restored to Eden (Figure 7.1[1]). We may question how much art is about beauty. Picasso's *Guernica* is not beautiful, but it is very truthful about the horrors of war. Nevertheless, there is no beauty without truth (and Wojtyła speaks of realism). The artist can educate the viewer to see the other person differently, to see more of the real, the truth. Molly Bythell's nude *where is the laptop* (see Chapter 3) does precisely this.

The celibate gaze: the transfiguration of desire?

Ola Sigurdson speaks of the loving as opposed to lustful gaze as a 'gaze for the invisible', as 'expectancy' (I believe there is more, that this person is more), rather than calculation. The Christian gaze attempts to establish a generous *relationship* to what it sees, as an indirect gaze on God (Sigurdson 2016, pp. 244, 250, 260, 288).

However, Sigurdson identifies chastity with sexual abstinence. This is of course the common use of the word, but in Roman Catholic theology at least it is understood differently. As a Dominican friar, I have taken a vow of *celibate* chastity, though more commonly people would call it simply 'chastity'. Karol Wojtyła's *Love and Responsibility* offers a strong model of chastity for the active and, above all, loving exercise of sexuality, for those who are called to this. But what might celibacy have to offer to the gaze? Or is it just a product of an immature, dualistic stage in Christian theology?

First, celibacy is advocated by Jesus himself as a possible but not universal vocation: 'Not everyone can accept this teaching, but only to those to whom it is given ... there are eunuchs who have made themselves eunuchs for the sake of the kingdom of heaven. Let anyone accept this who can' (Matt. 19.11–12). And we see that virginity was practised in the early Church by women (1 Cor. 7.25–38), but also by men (Rev. 14.4), including Paul himself (1 Cor. 7.7). Lived well, celibacy should free those called to it to love God with total freedom – including loving God in genuinely loving everyone and everything. While temperament and particular vocation may involve a greater or lesser solitude, the celibate, in his/her search for God, must be open to the other as gift. The great Orthodox hermit and spiritual guide St Seraphim of Sarov was remembered for his almost ecstatic greeting of visitors: 'My Joy! Christ is Risen!' They remembered too the blinding light of his face (Varden 2018, p. 128). Here was one who had been graced to share in the divine nature, and thus to see his brother or sister.

As Rowan Williams beautifully puts it, a basic task of Christian communities is to teach us 'to so order our relations that human beings may see themselves as desired, as the occasion of joy' (Williams 1996, p. 59). But to be truly formed by love of the human other, we need to know something of 'being the object of the causeless, loving delight of God', taking on the identity of God's child. So, Williams argues, our community 'needs some who are called beyond or aside from the ordinary patterns of sexual relation to put their identities directly into the hands of God in the single life' (p. 59). If this is not to be sterile, celibates need to know something about desiring and being desired. Their decision is 'to see if they can find themselves, their bodily selves, in a life dependent simply upon trust in the generous delight of God'. Williams sees this as 'a heavy task' but also fruitful in 'the great freedom of the celibate mystic in deploying the rhetoric of erotic love in speaking of God', and also an easy acceptance of the body, its needs and limitations, such as Teresa of Avila had in her last years (p. 65). This, Williams says, is essential background to understanding the body's grace. It has a paradoxical role in Christian community of 'the nourishing and enlarging of Christian sexuality' (p. 66).

Of course, such freedom and transformation are the fruit of a long pilgrimage of grace, of many spiritual battles. The safe distance which wears the face of pious detachment and chastity but actually fears engagement, vulnerability and the mutual gaze of love, is running away from ourselves: it is not chastity at all. Instead, this is the mask of the prude, as described by Wojtyła: it is denying the reality of his/her own sexuality and desire. Yet just as bad is the headlong embrace of the other that projects desire, projects an image on to the other and erases the brother's or sister's otherness, and can only end in serious hurt. It takes time to see the face of the other, and there will always be more to see. The distance of loving space nurtures the other, enables him or her to be themselves, and enables me to see them. The celibate could do well to ponder Emmanuel Levinas's words:

> But love also goes beyond the beloved. This is why through the face filters the obscure light coming from beyond the face, from what *is not yet,* from a future never future enough, more remote than the possible. (Levinas 1969, pp. 254–5)

The rules of religious communities have sought to put in place structures that would enable such a way of living. One of these is the *Rule of Saint Augustine*, still used by the Augustinian and Dominican orders. Augustine is remembered more for his sexual pessimism – for example, the lust which he compares to an ulcer of the soul in his *Confessions* – though admittedly this refers more to his misspent youth in Carthage, not to married life (Augustine, *Confessions* III.1/p. 55). And of course Augustine never had a Christian marriage, only an unstable relationship that eventually broke down. And he was an ex-barrister, a master of a rhetorical tradition that was expected to exaggerate in order to make its point. Augustine did not have English reserve. Yet this rhetoric is absent from his Rule, which does not make seeing a sin in itself. And it does insist that men are responsible for the chastity of their gaze just as much as women: chastity is required of men, not just women. So brothers going outside the house are reminded:

> When you see a woman, do not keep provocatively looking at her. Of course, no one can forbid you to see women

> when you go out, *but it is wrong to desire a woman or to want her to desire you* (cf. Matt 5.28) ... the eye is the herald of the heart. (*Rule of Saint Augustine* IV.4, pp. 16–18, my emphasis)

We should understand 'desire' in the sense of sexual desire not restrained and refocused by the will acting under God's grace.

And people see that we see (*Rule of Saint Augustine* IV.5), hence community members are responsible for nurturing the chaste gaze in each other (IV.6–11). What is most remarkable is that the admonition for the sisters is practically word-for-word the same (IV.1–11, pp. 29–32). Augustine's *Rule* is actually part of a larger theological vision. In *The City of God* he sees the great work as being the transformation of selfish love (*amor sui*) into love of God/God's love (*amor Dei*) (*City of God*, XIV.28/vol. 2, p. 410). Augustine looks forward to the new heaven and new earth in which we shall enjoy each other's beauty without any lust, actually rejoicing in the other's body. A transfigured desire through a transfigured gaze, like the icon ... Indeed, by the body we shall see God in every body (XXII.29/vol. 3, pp. 503–4), and 'these movements of our bodies will be of such unimaginable beauty' (XXII.30/vol. 3, p. 506). As Sigurdson says, the mystery of our body turns continually towards the invisible (Sigurdson 2016, p. 599). This does not mean a love that is kind but utterly impersonal, not seeing the person. Rather, it means that we will be graced to be real friends with everyone, seeing the depths and reality of the person that are now invisible. We can delight in them in their difference, for their own sake and for how this difference shows us a different aspect of God; think of Nicholas of Cusa's exercise with the gaze of the icon and the gaze on, and conversation with, the other brother (Chapter 6). The ban on 'particular friendships' traditionally imposed in celibate religious communities was not a ban on friendship as such, but on cliques, exclusive friendships: he/she is my friend but you're not.

Lived rightly, however, there is a sense in religious life of this gaze beginning now: Ambrose says to the consecrated virgin, 'You are one of God's people, one of the Church ... who enhance the grace of your body by the splendour of your soul' (Ambrose, *On Virginity* 12.68). We can and should delight in the other person's body, indeed seek out their beauty.

And in an early text which is perhaps the first Christian allegory, Hermas is welcomed with sisterly affection by the holy virgins who play and dance with him: he says that it was as if he had become young again (*The Shepherd of Hermas*, Similitude 9.2, 4).

There are losses in celibacy too. As we saw from Gregory Palamas, being embodied means that human beings share in God's creative nature by reproducing. By forgoing the active use of their sexuality, celibates, however nuptial their relationship with God may be, cannot share in the fundamental creativity of procreation, as well as not being able to experience bodily a complete intimacy with another person. Yet I suggest that in a hypersexualized age, an age when too often the body is desired and/or judged and the person is not seen, let alone loved, the purity of a mature celibate gaze offers the possibility of a gaze redeemed. If it has responded gracefully to the freedoms of friendship offered by modern society and modern Christianity, the celibate gaze offers a gentle reminder to the majority who are called to live their sexuality actively, that this must not be selfish, or even 'selfishness for two': rather a union of two, which is made possible by the opening to the third.

And, lived in God's grace, according to our different vocations, the erotic and celibate gazes come together as theotic gaze – a gaze that divinizes.

The theotic gaze

Remember how in Chapter 5 we read:

> The Lord is there and does not say, 'Look at me,' but, 'Look at the lilies of the field' ... The Word of God does not trample on creation, but rather, under his gaze of love, it appears in a dignity which is greater than royalty. (Hadjadj 2012, p. 61; cf. Matt. 6.28; Luke 12.27)

So Jesus looks in a way that actually draws the attention away from himself, while glorifying whatever he is looking at, showing it as it really is. The lilies appear in glory when Jesus casts his gaze of divine love on them – just as Jesus' appearance 'was made other' in his Transfiguration and he was revealed in his dazzling glory (Luke 9.29; Sigurdson 2016, p. 188).

In Chapters 5 and 6 we touched on divinization. According to 2 Peter 1.4, through God's gifts to us, especially his knowledge, God has given us his promises so that we 'may become participants in the divine nature (*theias koinonoi physeos*). This little phrase in 2 Peter is at the root of the great Eastern Christian theology of *theosis*, divinization: according to St Basil, one of the graces of the Holy Spirit is "becoming God"' (*On the Holy Spirit* 9.23/p. 44). It has become rather forgotten in the West, even though it is part of the Western theological tradition (see, for example, Aquinas, *Summa Theologiae*, I.ii.112.1). And in the Roman Rite of the Mass the priest says quietly while adding a drop of water to the wine as he prepares the gifts, 'Lord, by the mystery of this water and wine, may we come to share in the divinity of Christ who humbled himself to share in our humanity' (Roman Missal, p. 564). What is not so emphasized in the West is taken as normal in the East. In his classic work *The Mystical Theology of the Eastern Church*, Vladimir Lossky says (no doubt with an eye to Western nervousness in this regard):

> The words of St. Peter are explicit: *partakers of the divine nature*. They leave us in no doubt as to the reality of the union with God which is promised us, and set before us as our final end, the blessedness of the age to come. It would be childish, not to say impious, to see in these words only a rhetorical expression or metaphor. It would be altogether too facile to try to dispose of difficulty in this way, by emptying of their meaning whatsoever words of revelation do not readily correspond with our own modes of thought, which do not square with the idea of God which we have fashioned for ourselves. (Lossky 1976, pp. 67–8)

Of course, behind a certain Western nervousness one can see a desire to preserve the transcendence of God and to avoid the idol of 'self-spirituality'. Lossky is not unaware of this: following (Pseudo-?) Macarius (Homily 49, 155/816B), he affirms the absolute difference of the divine and human natures involved in union with God – otherwise, there would be nothing special about union with God. Yet this inaccessible God, who is already a communion as a Trinity of Father, Son and Holy Spirit, chooses to communicate himself to human beings.

Remarkably, Lossky says that although God can be known 'in creatures and by means of creatures ... He can also be known immediately in mystical contemplation, *in His uncreated energies which are the splendour of His face*' (Lossky 1976, p. 99), for example in the Transfiguration, when Peter, James and John see Christ shining with no earthly light. So it is that saints who abandon all things – because these things are *not* God – are taken up into union with God. Then they instantly 'possess in the same instant the knowledge of the whole world of being' (p. 99) – like St Benedict in his ecstasy, who saw 'the whole world ... gathered up before his eyes in what appeared to be a single ray of light' (Gregory the Great, *Dialogues* II.35/p. 105 – and remember Rabbi Ishmael's vision in Chapter 4). In other words, we see creation as God sees it – and by implication, we see others as God sees them, not distorted by our projections and comparisons to artificial standards, but rather as they really are. Then, like Moses reflecting the divine light as he came down from the mountain, we reflect God's light, God's love, on those we gaze upon, *because we see God in them, the image and likeness*. Our gaze is no less personal:

> The personal character of a human being who has entered on the way of union is never impaired, even though he renounces his own will and his natural inclinations' – rather, this is the way by which 'the human personality comes to its full realization in grace. What is not free and definitely conscious has no personal value. (Lossky 1976, p. 217)

And seeing God in the other is not to disembody them. It is to see *this* person, body and soul. As Fabrice Hadjadj so beautifully puts it, overcoming the immaturity and unchastity of the past, 'From now on I can gaze on my wife's body no longer as a temptation, but as an icon' (Hadjadj 2012, p. 171, my translation).

We do not know what God is, we cannot define God, we can only conceive of the image of God in the human being. What is clear, though, is that, 'Creation in the image and likeness of God implies the idea of participation in the divine Being, of communion with God. That is to say, it presupposes grace' (Lossky 1976, p. 118). By grace, the divine image and likeness are realized in us: the tarnish is removed so that the icon may shine. And the gaze of divine love that Christians are called to mediate is part of that work.

Christ divinizes us. And Christians look on others in his Name. I would like to suggest that our gaze at others, at their embodied selves, can be divinizing: a *theotic gaze*. When Peter and John looked on a beggar in Christ's name, they healed him (Acts 3.1–7). A purified, graced gaze, which has heeded the philosopher's call to see the face of the other, embraced chastity and has also been saved from the trap of idolatry by not making the other their god, can gaze with delight, love and compassion. This delight, mirrored in a dialogue of eyes, may be the beginnings of a truly erotic love, or the beginnings of a friendship, or a fleeting moment of one stranger helping another off the train, when the gaze of one or both is the beginning of a transformation lasting long after the goodbye. The photographer's light in the *WE ARE WOMEN* exhibition (see Chapter 3) preserves for us a gaze that delights in others, sees them as they really are, and reveals their glory.

Note

1 All images are available to view online at: https://scmpress.hymnsam.co.uk/media/74923/images-for-how-do-i-look.pdf.

8

The Tribe of the Seers

Heaven or earth, God or people?

'I'm not a mystic, I'm down to earth' (literally, 'I'm in life'), says Agnès Varda in *Faces Places* (see Chapter 3). In a film that sees so well and with such compassion and generosity, there is still a contradiction implied between the mystic and the person living in the world. It is clearly not enough simply to disagree, to come up with counter-examples. Foucault teaches us (Chapter 2) that what we call knowledge has not just reasoning behind it but history: what he calls genealogies. Beliefs interact with the changes, sometimes violent, of history. And these changes change the beliefs, and so in turn new beliefs come about. The beliefs always have reasons behind them, such as advances in understanding of medicine and of crime. But the subjective elements cannot be taken away. Assumptions are made in the midst of real science. Assumptions about the importance (or not) of care by loved ones for the healing of a sick person; assumptions about the legitimacy of norms of behaviour. A norm may change, but a practice continues. For example, interventional state surveillance on behaviour has greatly reduced since the social revolutions of the 1960s, but unaccountable organizations are harvesting vast amounts of data about you and me through our computers, even through the tiny dot of the computer camera. Not to mention the CCTV camera. So we feel watched, and act accordingly.

Likewise with life values and beliefs, which include not only religious but also agnostic and atheistic perspectives. So, in Agnès Varda's remark, there are genealogies. The concept of the mystic is set against the person in everyday life. The mystic is seen as someone withdrawn from people and from personal relationships, cold and distant, a person only interested in heaven and suspicious of the 'distraction' of 'creatures'. The contrast is the person in life. In Agnès Varda's contrast there are shades of the characters in Albert Camus's *The Plague*: the severe Father Paneloux, who thunders from the pulpit that the plague is a deserved punishment, versus the humane Dr Rieux, who does what he can for the victims and seeks only human tenderness. When Fr Paneloux witnesses the horrible death of the child of one of his most devout parishioners and allies, he changes his tune, instead engaging in tending the sick and, concerning God, simply saying that perhaps we can love what we can't understand. Camus (1913–60) was not religious as such, but neither was he anti-Christian (see Lottman 1979, pp. 290–1). Yet with his humanistic focus, he was clearly more convinced by the model of the socially engaged priest.

And so it happened in the French Catholic Church and elsewhere between the 1960s and the 1980s, especially with the impetus of the social revolution of 1968, with its emphasis on individual and bodily freedom, especially the freedom of women, and on social issues. Agnès Varda took an enthusiastic part in 1968 (see her film *The Beaches of Agnès*, 2008). However, many, often younger, Catholics are now critical of this approach, feeling that worship has become despiritualized. They may seek more traditional forms of worship that are more about silence and worship, in which participation and community are more implicit than explicit. An example of more changes in belief in response to events and circumstances.

This suggests that we will never be able to reduce the Christian gaze beyond the search for the face of God and the face of our neighbour. It suggests that the mystic has to be in life and also life must not forget the mystical dimension. We have seen that the gaze is a shared concern of Christians and others. Christianity is not merely about the great hereafter: Jesus never separates salvation from ethical behaviour, and indeed shows that ethical behaviour is part of conversion: 'Love your neighbour as yourself' (Mark 12.31); 'love one another. Just as I have loved you' (John 13.34).

But there is an innocence about Agnès Varda, a veteran film maker who works with a young artist inhabiting the world of the selfie, yet does not retouch people's pictures. She has no answer to the problem of shy Nathalie's huge poster image going viral on social media as people take selfies with it and Nathalie becoming the emblem of a small town, to her own discomfort. Things have moved on. There has been a birth of new beliefs about the image, one's own image. Before social media, people would still have looked at the poster of Nathalie, still taken photos, maybe of themselves with it. The photos would have found their way into photo albums, family slide shows, maybe magazines. Nathalie might still have been uncomfortable with this. But with social media, her image becomes the subject of instant, massive and uncontrollable dissemination. Not to mention the comments that people might be making on social media about her image.

Anxiety about one's appearance is of course ancient. We saw in Chapter 1 that there have always been ideal standards of beauty in every society, such as the statues of ancient Greece. Human beings compare themselves with others, rate themselves and others, despise or envy others, more often secretly despise themselves. The necessary but practically impossible task is to stop people comparing themselves with others (Tiggemann and McGill 2004, p. 40; see Chapter 1). But bring the camera together with the internet, the mobile phone and photo retouching technology, and things are brought to a new level. The impossibly perfect image of ourselves that we can post on social media becomes the reality because it looks like it's the reality. We know it's not, of course, and the result is an outbreak of low self-image, anxiety and body dysmorphia, especially among teenagers and young adults, who are the greatest users of photo-sharing social media (Kelly et al. 2019; see Chapter 1).

So this is a genealogy: just as people have children, and they in turn have children who are like their parents and grandparents as well as being different and new, so with the issues of the image and the gaze. There is a constant, a transmission, yet to each generation it brings new problems in response to developments in society and technology.

Traces of a response

In this book we have traced a possible Christian response. Starting with wisdom already present in philosophy, we have seen the enduring clinical gaze and gaze of surveillance in Foucault; the potentially negative impact of another's presence in my field of vision (Sartre), though also the potential opening of new possibilities through their presence (Mounier); the 'mirror phase' (the child realizing that it's themselves they see in the mirror, and thus that they can be seen) and the erotic gaze, as well as the issue of shame (being seen looking, or thinking we might be seen) in Lacan. We saw how Laura Mulvey exposed the male gaze in classic cinema, which tends to deprive women of being subjects; and the radically different philosophy of the gaze of Emmanuel Levinas, who argues for the absolute priority of the ethical demand that the face of the other person places on me and, in his discussion of the 'saying' between faces, shows the inspiration of Israel's search for the face-to-face vision of God and the importance of the word and the hearing and speaking of conversation.

Artists also had resources for us on the gaze: Agnès Varda's film *Faces Places*; the different gaze made visible in Molly Bythell's painting *where is the laptop*; the active subjects who work with the photographer to construct the gaze in *WE ARE WOMEN*; and the mysterious Holy Face of Tours, possibly originating in an image not made with human hands: Christ in his passion with his eyes closed, the death of the gaze, and yet the working of miracles ...

In the Jewish Scriptures, the Old Testament, we found the universal question of vision being answered with Israel's search for the face of God, a gaze that is mutual and transformative. The seer is transformed by seeing God, being seen by God in the shining light of his face, and then seeing him/herself as they truly are: the verb of seeing in reciprocal, reflexive and transformative Middle Voice. Yet the problem of the idol was also present, and was a tension within the Jewish tradition, seeing versus hearing. The idol is an omnipresent problem, our own image or an image we create projected on to God and others.

Jesus, the Word of God made flesh, sees people in a mutual gaze that transforms them, and looks lovingly into the truth of who each person is. And Jesus teaches an ethic of a loving, chaste gaze in which no one is a bystander, but, rather, we may gaze on our neighbour with transforming love.

The early Church knew the vision of Christ in glory (Stephen, John in Revelation). The early Christian ritual of baptism, in which the candidates were reborn to share in God's nature (*theosis*, divinization, 2 Peter 1.4), also included being seen as transformed and glorified. By anointing with oil, the new Christian's face shone physically, to a dazzling level when reflecting the light of the rising sun or of lamps: shining like the Lord in glory, and seeing others behold one in that state (we will return to this below). Those examples of saints who became radiant; and, in the Letter of James, the possibility of early Christians gazing on an icon of the Lord like a mirror in which they saw themselves transformed – and with strong ethical implications for ongoing conversion of one's way of life.

We looked more deeply into the theology of the icon, and the veneration of Christ's real presence in the Eucharist. We discovered that we see, and yet do not see, so we cannot make an idol. The icon, indeed, reverses the perspective, the looking, from the transfigured state of heaven into our world, transforming us. Whereas Susan Sontag saw death in the photograph, because it captured a lost moment in the lives of people who were ageing and dying, the icon sees us from eternity. So we can see the photograph as giving us back time, time to see in the moment what we missed about a person that we will encounter again in eternity. We found that in the Eucharist we see Christ present, and yet because we do not see him as he actually appears in glory, there is a distance that draws us to the consummation, when we shall see him face to face. We found too that his real presence saves us from demanding too much of God in the other person, and that this graces us to look on our brother, our sister, our neighbour, made in God's image, as icon and presence of God. We receive God's presence in them while not making a god out of them – and we see them as themselves. Listening, as well as seeing, is essential to relationship: the example of Nicholas of Cusa's multimedia *Vision of God* brings together the gaze of God and the gaze of/on our brother or sister, and a conversation with them about what they have seen.

We looked too at the integration of the erotic gaze. Jesus' teaching on the lustful eye is very strict: and while an uncritical use of Platonist philosophy, with its body-denying tendencies, undoubtedly had a negative influence on early Christian theology, the hypersexualization of our culture has also been found destructive, with damage to body image when bodies are treated as 'successful' or 'unsuccessful' (Ammicht-Quinn 2009, pp. 72–4). Seeing the body but not the person ...

Drawing on the Theology of the Body of Karol Wojtyła (St John Paul II), born of his work with married couples, we see a joyful acceptance of attraction, which finds its integration in loving the person, on relationship, so that they know that they experience being seen as being loved. The transfiguration of desire in those called to celibacy for the sake of the Kingdom of Heaven seeks God everywhere and is open to receiving love from everyone and giving love to everyone. Rooted in the knowledge that God delights in us and that we are loved, celibacy offers a gentle challenge to a hypersexualized society, to step back from the immediate fulfilment of sexual desire and to see the person in the fullness of their beauty. In Christ, erotic and celibate gazes together become theotic: delighting in the other person, not calculating but seeking the more that is there – that is, them. Seeing the divine image, including in the person's suffering, and not drawing attention to ourselves and the person as the solution to my needs, but instead receiving their gift to us and reflecting back the person's glory as made in God's image. Receiving as gift, it may indeed open a conversation, a saying between faces that are starting to see each other. It may become an erotic relationship and eventually a marriage, or a friendship, or even that brief encounter that nevertheless remains in us as a sign of eternal life.

Where sin is clearly visible in the person's actions, by God's grace we can still see the divine image, albeit tarnished: we are all sinners, and even in the worst cases, there but for the grace of God go I. Sister Helen Préjean, working with death row prisoners, draws out the beauty and goodness beyond the sin. Through her prayer, patience and love, she brings Christ's redemption to hitherto murderous and unrepentant criminals, revealing their beauty (see the film *Dead Man Walking* (1995), based on a true story).

On being seen

When I started writing this book, my main preoccupation was the crisis of the gaze in the world and how redemptive it is that Christians believe that everyone is made in God's image and likeness. So we encounter God in each and every person – what a gift this is to us, and what a gift to them in a world of judging gazes. Of course, Christians have failed to gaze lovingly, we do judge. But surely, with a bit of repentance and with divine grace, we have a wonderfully redemptive gift for the world, with no words required. An easy preaching in a world that rejects the religious word?

But then I realized that to see, we need to know first, to have experienced, being seen by God, by his gaze. We cannot give what we have not got. And many Christians struggle with low self-esteem. Because ours is a religion of Incarnation, of God taking flesh and living in the world, we live in the world, in our particular places and cultures, and look just like other people. We do not have special clothes or diets that set us apart. So we experience the same problems as others, and we too are hurt by judging and contemptuous gazes. In the face of all that, Christians too struggle with self-image: we too are crucified by selfie culture. We may also be guilty of judging and contemptuous gazes. Many of us are active on social media (not least because it is an easy way to gather the Church and reach the unchurched). And we also get hurt by the nasty comments, if we do not also make them ourselves. Part of the mystery of our living in the world is that it is God's creation in its beauty and goodness, and yet it is fallen. So we are influenced simultaneously for good and ill, simultaneously we receive gifts and are broken. This is true even of those Christians God calls to live apart from the world in hidden lives of prayer, in religious communities, who are at the heart of the Church, praying for the needs of all the Church and the whole world, interceding for the poor, the wounded, the victims of war, the violated, and for their tormentors. And it does not take long living in a religious community to understand that the line between good and evil runs not between the Church and the world, but through the human heart.

There are further challenges for Christians, especially young Christians, in becoming a minority in what had once been a Christian country. A very imperfectly Christian country, but one where certain cultural assumptions – about rights and duties, about relationships, but most basically of all, that going to church on Sunday was normal – have been eroded or forgotten. If you're a student, you might find yourself having to choose between a weekend field trip or student society excursion, and going to church. Religion, especially Christianity, can be treated with contempt by one's peers, and a cultural default of scientific materialism (only what we can see is real) shuts down the possibility of dialogue. Although scientific materialism has been a cultural factor in universities for over a hundred years, its normalization, and indeed its aggressive character in society in general, is evidence of growing tribalism, an issue that we will address later.

All these things I have started to see through my pastoral experience as a priest, and especially as I reflect on the seven years I spent until recently as a chaplain to students. Catholic (and other) students valued the safe space of our Catholic Chaplaincy which, for all the inevitable imperfections and hiccups, was a community that sought to welcome unconditionally. But a good number seemed to experience the Christian lifestyle and its expectations of religious practice and morality, especially around chastity, as a burden, an impossible to-do list, and indeed an invitation to being attacked, rather than a joy and liberation. Add to this the shattering revelations of abuse in Christian families and by clergy, of which young

Christians themselves can be victims, and the exhortation to look on others with a theotic gaze may feel like one job too many. Can't I just come to church when I can, pray when I can, try to be a good person, and volunteer in the soup kitchen once a week? Christian self-confidence and self-esteem can, in reality, be very low.

Of course, issues over the body and self-image are not confined to Christianity. It seems that it's a universal problem that's always been there and which the culture of the social image has exacerbated. It was from students and other young adults of all religions and none that I learnt how the swimming pool, the gym and the beach had become places of real body anxiety. But it's not enough for Christians to say, 'The world has the same problem.' If we can't offer some answer, some healing, then why be a Christian? What difference does it make?

For this reason I think that for our own healing, our own *self-gaze*, we need to have experienced being gazed on with a divine, theotic gaze. A rich theology of being made in God's image, the Incarnation and Resurrection of Jesus, being saved, is all well and good, but it appeals primarily to the mind. We are made embodied by God: knowledge comes to us through our senses. So how can we experience the divine gaze in our bodies?

If my reading of baptism is correct (Chapter 5), the first Christians emerged from the rite of baptism with faces shining with anointing oil, and then saw the rising sun and/or an image of the Lord in candlelight. With the sun or candlelight shining on them, their faces were dazzling to their brothers and sisters who saw them (compare modern make-up), and they would have seen the others' gaze on them. They would have seen people seeing them glorified, *beautiful*. An experience of being loved (see Chapter 5). As they heard the Word of God more, and went through post-baptismal instruction, they would come to understand that their experience was that of becoming physically like the appearance of the glorified Lord, in whose divine nature they now shared. Of course, it didn't mean instant holiness: we still sin after baptism, but we have embarked on the journey of holiness (see Romans 6—8) and been given a foretaste of what we will become. In the struggles of our vocation, lived out in an ordinary human life with its joys and sorrows, the memory of a powerful somatic experience of transformation, of being seen and loved, is always a resource to draw on, a source of resilience, an 'anti-trauma' if you like. But we cannot remember what we have not experienced.

Especially in an age so body-centred and body-conflicted, is it not time that we recovered this ancient rite? As many or most Christians are baptized as babies (though this may change in this secular age), most of us can't remember our baptisms. For cultural reasons, the rite of baptism has become very attenuated in most places – just a few drops of water and a couple of dabs of oil, although some communities still practise immersion. But perhaps we could recover the ancient tradition in the context of a retreat in which, without any pretence of rebaptism – for our dying and rising in Christ is once and for all – we return to this moment through physical ritual. A friend is planning a retreat centre which could incorporate this as what she calls the 'embodied sacred'.

And then to look on our neighbour with a theotic gaze would not be one more thing I have to do. It would simply come, *radiate,* from our being, from what we had experienced by God's grace. We would know that our image does not need to be 'retouched' to be successful. We are made in God's image, and God does not need retouching.[1] So the difference and diversity of the other person replaces comparison. Each person, a different and complementary image of God.

Sharing the gaze

But I also envisage two possibilities, a workshop and an interactive exhibition, to help Christians and non-Christians alike to engage actively with the theotic gaze. First, a workshop on the gaze that is being developed by a friend who is an artist and spiritual director. People are seated at tables, opposite one another. The first step is with the written word: writing a favourite prayer or scriptural verse to God or, for the non-religious, something inspirational that connects them with what they regard as the higher or divine. They can do it in any shape, but must not remove the pen from the paper while writing. The next stage is to look at an icon (original or print, but a real icon, not just any picture, let alone the so-fragile 'icons' of celebrity), which is given at random, face down, to be shared by pairs of participants sitting next to one another. We spend time looking at the icon in silence – 'beholding', we might say – and then 'writing' on it with our mind's pen the words we have received from contemplating the icon, what it has revealed to us. Then each person is seen by and looks at the person opposite them. One person closes their eyes and is seen by the other as an icon, 'beholding' them and then 'writing' on their face the words they received from contemplating the icon. The other as icon ... (see Chapter 6).

There is no 'group sharing' afterwards. How people respond is up to them. At a workshop I attended, though, I was impressed by the light and the smile of the person opposite me after we had finished, and the quality and depth of the conversation over lunch. It was something gentle.

This book started as a review of some art exhibitions (White 2017), written in the light of Fabrice Hadjadj's book, which I was reading at the time. Now, having written the book, I have an idea for another art exhibition. A travelling, interactive exhibition of paintings and photographs (and possibly video) that offer challenging, different, wholesome gazes, and a new relationship with self-image in social media.

An exhibition version of this book would use prints of original paintings and photographs (such as Molly Bythell's work and the *WE ARE WOMEN* photographs discussed in Chapter 3), which could be sent by email as high-definition files, to minimize costs. The exhibition would be installed at places of recreation often experienced as sites of body anxiety and pain in the age of the selfie and the successful/unsuccessful body: gyms, swimming pools and beaches. Visitors would be invited to take a selfie before they entered. On entry, they would be required to deposit their phone and any other photographic device in a secure locker, for which they would be given a key on a wristband. The lockers would be out of sight of the gym, pool or beach: in the case of open-air pools and beaches, a fence would be erected around the space, its impact inside softened with plants (like the medieval 'garden enclosed'). Once inside the exhibition, visitors would be able to use the gym, pool or beach as normal. But they would be without their phones: so no selfies or photos of others. They could of course return to access their phones at any time, but only outside the enclosure.

The exhibition would offer a positive gaze where one major temptation to a negative gaze, the phone camera, had been taken away. Of course, people can still look with judgement or lust without a phone, and images form our gaze. But *because* images form our gaze, the exhibition – placed so that people would necessarily encounter the images as they made use of the space – would offer them positive gazes. Given also that phones provide an acceptable form of 'social fiddling' – as the cigarette culture once did, now thankfully in the past – board games might be provided, nature trails at beaches and natural pools, and/or a simple pop-up café with bench tables to encourage social interaction. Clearly, the exhibition would need attendants who would be trained to deal with any inappropriate behaviour.

On leaving the exhibition, and upon reclaiming their phone, people would be encouraged to take another selfie and compare it with the one they had taken before entering. They would be able to post these on the exhibition's social media, along with thoughts and comments (subject to moderation). So social media would not be denied, but its excesses and failings could be redeemed.

The exhibition could also take place in conjunction with the workshop I described above. And I welcome a conversation with artists, curators, activists and potential venues, and also with psychologists and counsellors, as initial discussions have shown a need for support to be on hand in case people who are vulnerable around self- or body image have an adverse reaction. There could also be an opportunity for healing in this.

The Tribe of the Seers

Agnès Varda died in March 2019. I wonder what she sees now, no longer feeling the contradiction between mysticism and life? But I suspect she would still urge us to be down to earth, to apply the gaze. It has become more urgent. Agnès died at a time when her beloved Paris was being convulsed by riots against the government. Britain was polarized over Brexit, and at the time of writing (2020) it is not clear how the gulf between Leavers and Remainers will be healed. Many politicians have resigned over the torrents of insults and threats they receive on social media. The Far Right is on the rise across Europe, even in Germany and in liberal Sweden. Nothing looks certain any more, we are not listening to the other, seeing them and their point of view, and the culture of democratic consensus is dying. We have become a society of tribes and populist autocrats are increasingly admired. And amid all this, the planet is literally on fire in Australia and other places.

Society is, I would suggest, being replaced by tribes, chiefly marked by politics or wealth, and increasingly by ethnicity or religion. The liberal individualist model has failed because we don't have enough to hold us together. We lived for a couple of generations on the capital of Christendom – but now it's been used up. Just what ethical basis do we have for loving our neighbour, feeding the poor, healing the sick, treating the weak and suffering with compassion? There is still a lot of goodwill, individuals and groups engaged in wonderful projects for the poor and the environment. But it is fragile and easily broken by disagreement. More tribes. Not that Christians have not, shamefully, warred and broken apart. But we have a common source to return to, in which to be reunited. Much progress has been made on this, by God's grace.

But faced with tribalism, it is not surprising that many Christians want (unlike their parents' generation) *more* distinctive identity, *more* things that set them apart from society. Two generations ago British Catholics abandoned the ghetto to embrace the world, to stop looking different (see the novels of David Lodge, such as *How Far Can You Go?* and *The British*

Museum is Falling Down). Now a sizeable proportion of their practising Catholic grandchildren want more distinctively Catholic things: more eucharistic adoration, more Rosary, more Latin Masses. Because, without identifiers, who are we? Who am I? Where, in this lonely world, do I belong? Which is my tribe?

But does that make Catholics, or Christians in general, one tribe among many? It could do. And if it makes us fail in the basic step of loving our neighbour, fail to recognize God in the other person, it is not Christian, and must be opposed.

But Christians could become a different type of tribe. We could 'baptize' tribalism. We could become a tribe of those who see others with love, whose gaze is transformative, because we ourselves have experienced being seen by God's love. To see the other, to converse, to invite them into our communities, is to fulfil the literal meaning of religion – 're-binding' – the work of Jesus, binding back together what is broken. We can be involved in all good projects – ecological activism, anti-bullying measures in schools that emphasize difference, and work on emotional literacy. We cannot expect instant transformation, and things may get a lot worse before they get better, which is one reason why we need our tribe to retreat to at times, where we can be seen and heard in the mutual gaze of divine love.

Then we can go out again, and many of our performances of the theotic gaze will be everyday and unplanned, prompted in the secret of our hearts by the Holy Spirit. Such as this true story told me by a Christian colleague who gave me essential help with this book. She used to run a Christian hostel in Amsterdam, on the edge of the red light district. One day she got into conversation with a female sex worker. After a while the woman said to her, 'You're a Christian, aren't you?'

'How do you know?'

'Because you look me in the eye.'

Note

1 I am indebted to Mia Fox for this observation.

Postscript

The Gaze After Covid-19

I'm finishing this book under lockdown during the Covid-19 pandemic of 2020. Obviously, I can have little idea of how things will be when this book is published, and I can have even less idea of how they will be when you're reading these words months or years later. Perhaps the world will have changed beyond recognition to a 'new normal'. Perhaps it won't have changed at all. Perhaps something in-between. But when a crisis comes – such as in time of plague or other natural disaster, or war, or personal tragedy – it's not primarily about the event that precipitates the crisis, but rather, how we respond to the crisis. The word 'crisis' literally means 'judgement'. For some Christians, the pandemic is God's judgement on an immoral and unbelieving world (cf. the plagues in Revelation 6.8 and chapters 15—16). Others strongly disagree, pointing out how many innocent people have died. Pope Francis, addressing the world alone from a rainy St Peter's Square, said that Covid-19 is not God's judgement on us, but rather that God is inviting *us* to judge what is important to us. God calls us to repentance not so that he can condemn us, but so that we can experience repentance, *metanoia* – that is, have a change of heart, come to a new judgement – and accept the gift of salvation. That is the true crisis.

So, reflecting on the Pope's words, I think I need to apply the particular issues that the crisis of the pandemic has raised to our discussion of the gaze. However the world changes or doesn't change following Covid-19, the real tragedy would be to have 'had the experience and missed the meaning', in the words of the poet T. S. Eliot. So what do the lasting lessons

.that God might be offering us through the pandemic mean for our understanding of the gaze – whether or not a 'second wave' comes or not, or fresh pandemics come, or other disasters?

Let's look first at how our gaze has changed during the pandemic.

In a society that seemed to be falling apart, dividing into tribes, there has been a resurgence of community spirit and sacrifice: people calling and shopping for their neighbours, families reuniting around WhatsApp and Zoom calls. Health workers have been heroic in caring for the sick, some of them also getting ill and even dying in the process. New hospitals have been built in record time, the government has poured in cash, aided by a 100-year-old war veteran who raised £33 million by walking laps of his garden.

There has also been division. Some people feel that the government acted too slowly and that it is now easing restrictions too fast, others that the restrictions have done more harm – to the economy and mental health – than good. Isolating people – especially the over-seventies, who are subject to the severest restrictions – is certainly not good for mental health. And we risk being separated into generational tribes.

And others are afraid to go out even with lockdown being eased.

We said we cared about the environment, and carefully recycled, telling ourselves that this would somehow rebalance those car and plane trips. With most aeroplanes grounded and land traffic drastically reduced, carbon emissions have fallen significantly and the air in our towns and cities is noticeably cleaner. The ducks are wandering around Cambridge and a badger is now a frequent visitor to our garden.

Seeing most of those dear to us has been only by computer or phone screen. Before, we were physically together but often looking at our screens rather than one another. We tortured ourselves and one another about our appearance, when we could 'retouch' our photo and then struggle in vain to look like the unreal people on the screen. Now, seeing one another by screen, we long to see the real person in the flesh. Physical 'imperfection' suddenly seems irrelevant.

And our relationship with our own bodies has changed. With lockdown enclosing my life at home and forcibly disembodying me by on-screen interaction, I have felt impelled to take much more exercise, rather than putting it off because I had 'more important' things to do, and have so much appreciated nature and how it is blooming as I run around a lake.

In our households, we are obliged to spend more time together, negotiating common time and also personal space. We cannot ignore each other or run away any more. New friendships have started, old loves have rekindled, but some relationships have run into serious strain. Children often find the confinement especially hard. Relationships of convenience are no longer possible – couples have had to choose either to live together or live apart. For dating Christian couples who are committed to the traditional teaching of pre-marital abstinence, this has been especially challenging.

With places of worship closed, many more people than physically attended before are taking part by live streaming, TV or radio. From my community we are reaching the whole world, even people in prison, and I have started preparing someone in Trinidad for baptism. But Christians are so hungry to receive the Body of Christ, and we miss being the Body of Christ together. Yet when we were together, how often were we bored or not present to the Word of God, the Eucharist, our brother or sister? How often did the clergy moan about 'the people' – suddenly missing you when you're no longer here with us and we have to do the whole service ourselves? Yet many Christians have put aside disagreement and instead embraced this as a time of God calling the world on retreat: to sit still, to be present, and to be alone. I have received astonishing testimonies of inner healing and spiritual transformation, of a much greater and more global sense in isolation of being community, of being church. Jean-Luc Marion had reflected on the importance of distance, so that we don't think we have 'arrived' and 'got' the God who is present, but not yet come in glory (see Chapter 6).

Our wider community: we speak so much about community, but have we really engaged with our community – especially with the poor? Suddenly a lot of homeless people have been put up in hotels. And with the universal risk of infection, and the restrictions of lockdown, society has been levelled – at least to some extent, although poverty inevitably impacts on health and immunity, and furloughing and aid are not universally distributed. In many developing countries, lockdown is a luxury, if you have enough space and enough personal resources.

When we go out, we have to negotiate others. There have been new smiles of appreciation as we give each other physical space: but also looks of fear – that other person could infect me. Perhaps the smile is sometimes a mask for the fear. Then the mask – to wear or not to wear, the mask that hides the face, that hides me, hides you? How can I smile with my mouth covered? My smile must be as much about my eyes as my mouth – no longer just an automatic facial movement.

For Emmanuel Levinas, philosopher of the face (see Chapter 2), the touch, the caress, not just the gaze and the conversation, are part of our encounter with the other person. For Thomas Aquinas, touch is the *sensus communis*, the 'common sense', literally, the only sense where our body is in actual contact with the object of our perception. But now we're careful what we touch and how we touch it. And whom we touch. No handshakes, no hugs or kisses. But when we shook hands, was it a sign of openness and trust, or just a convention? Was the hug or kiss a sign of love, or just what you do in a friendship group? Did it meet my need for touch more than expressing my love for you? And as for sexual contact, how loving, how meaningful was the most intimate thing you can do?

We need to touch and be touched. We need to sing together. And fear is bad for us. Already some people are afraid to go out and take even the physical space and social encounter to which they're entitled. And how can we be church together if we still have to sit at distance? Receive Holy Communion? Sing 'psalms and hymns and spiritual songs' (Eph. 5.19)? How can community meetings and democracy operate if numbers are restricted by space? Yes, we can do a lot online (if the internet is working properly), but much of our communication depends on body language too.

If God has called us on retreat, we need to trust him that he will bring us back. But the whole point of a retreat is a journey of conversion, not just coming back to the 'same old same old'. This is *metanoia*, usually translated as 'repentance', but its deep meanings are thinking about things differently, a change of heart and of direction, an entering into the meta-mind (i.e. the mind of God). There has been much talk of a 'new normal'. *To be Christian is always to be orientated towards a 'new normal'*. That new normal is the Resurrection, the risen life that we put on in baptism. The task of fully embracing this risen life is our Christian discipleship, a lifelong work, truly a work of repentance, always being open to a change of heart, to coming to a new judgement. St Paul charts this in Romans 6—8: it is a work that can only happen by the Holy Spirit's grace working within us. I am particularly reminded of this truth because I'm writing these words during the 'novena' of Pentecost, the nine days of special prayer to the Holy Spirit between the feasts of the Ascension of the Lord and Pentecost.

How, then, can the Spirit lead us back? In the present circumstances, it's ironic that the biblical words for Spirit (Hebrew *ruach*, Greek *pneuma*) literally mean *breath* – as in the hymn, *Breathe on me, breath of God*. Covid-19 causes an often vicious respiratory illness, one of whose symptoms is struggling to breathe. Fear is, of course, bad for our breathing: we tend to breathe more shallowly when we're anxious, which makes it harder for us to expel toxins – and this puts us at more risk of falling ill. But early Christian baptism was, on a bodily level, an experience of deep breaths. The baptismal candidate was plunged into cold water. When you come out of cold water you naturally breathe in deeply and sharply. So receiving in baptism the 'breath', the Spirit of God whom Jesus had breathed over his disciples (John 20.22), would have been a very physical experience. The Christian was to be a 'spiritual' (*pneumatikos*) person, able 'to discern all things'. Early Christians were to pray 'lifting up holy hands' (1 Tim. 2.8), as some still do today. Raising the hands and arms, as we see in early Christian art, opens the chest to breathe.

If early Christian initiation and prayer were good for the

health, they also belonged to a Christian context that experienced real bodily healing: Jesus healed people, so did the first Christians (such as Peter healing Aeneas, Acts 9.32–33). 'Save' and 'heal' are actually the same word in the Greek of the New Testament, *sozein*: 'Get up and go on your way,' said Jesus to the leper, 'your faith has saved/healed you' (Luke 17.19, my translation). (And note that 'get up' is the same as 'rise', as in the Resurrection.)

Since then saints have continued to heal in Jesus' name, by the power of the Holy Spirit. Whole communities and religious orders have also been raised up who dedicate themselves to the care of the sick and the dying. But as the centuries have gone by, have we Christians become more anxious to avoid illness than to embrace wellness? Is our faith sometimes only a prop? Do we fear being healed (on every level) when our sickness and neurosis keep us safe?

This is not in any way to say that if you're sick it must be your fault. Nor to deny the real apostolate of the sick and suffering. Saints like Thérèse of Lisieux, whom we encountered in this book, and Elizabeth of the Trinity, died young from illness. They, like St Paul, and very knowingly, carried in their bodies 'what is lacking in Christ's afflictions for the sake of his body, that is, the church' (Col. 1.24). In union with Jesus, they carried the sufferings of their weaker brothers and sisters. But they were not malingerers: they were fully alive. They had already died and risen in baptism, fully embraced the Resurrection, and were full of the Spirit: Thérèse and Elizabeth were already great spiritual teachers in their early twenties. St Catherine of Siena (1347–80) healed victims of the plague in her city, though she died young of illness herself. She had long overcome any fear of death.

This doesn't mean either that Christians don't need medicine or should ignore true science. All truth comes from God: 'the truth will make you free' (John 8.32), and discerning that truth is part of living a truly 'spiritual' life. So we might be surprised at what medical science has actually discovered. Dr Gabor Maté, a general practitioner in a poor quarter of Vancouver, had a gift of attentive listening. Beyond the obvious discovery that illness is often caused by stress, he started noticing correlations between types of illness and personality types. For example, he found that people with auto-immune diseases, which are difficult to treat, were often over-independent personalities, unwilling or suspicious of accepting help and love. Experience had turned them in on themselves – just as, in an auto-immune disease, the immune system turns inwards and attacks the body. Maté also found that when people started to realize this, and he was able to help them have a change of heart ('repent') and start to accept care and love, they started to heal (Maté 2019). 'This is just how I am' is simply not true. And if it is not true even at a 'secular' level, it is even less true at a level of Christian faith, when Jesus calls us to repentance so that we can receive his healing salvation. My own experience of a complete healing from asthma has proven to me how Christ 'baptizes' medicine and therapy with the grace of repentance – a change of heart and entering into the mind of God, starting to breathe with the Breath of God.

So I suggest it's time for us Christians to rediscover Christ's healing (with all the 'dealing with one's stuff' that that involves), and to breathe with the Spirit. With Christ's love dwelling in us through the Holy Spirit, we will live without fear. Our gaze will then be a healing gaze, our breath a healing breath. Community and the touch of love will become more real, rooted in the healing Christ and breathing the life-giving Spirit, together singing creation's praise of God.

> May the God of peace himself sanctify you entirely; and may your spirit and soul and body be kept sound and blameless at the coming of our Lord Jesus Christ. (1 Thess. 5.23)

Bibliography

Primary sources

Agnès de Jésus (Marie-Pauline Martin), *Yellow Notebook* (*Cahier Jaune*), Archives du Carmel de Lisieux, www.archives-carmel-lisieux.fr/carmel/index.php/carnet-jaune/2320-carnet-jaune (accessed 28 November 2019).

Ambrose, *De Virginitate* ['On Virginity'], Egnatius Cazzaniga (ed.), Turin: G.B. Paravia & Co., 1948; translation of XII.68 in *The Divine Office: The Liturgy of the Hours According to the Roman Rite*, vol. 1, London & Glasgow: Collins, 1974, pp. 36–7.

Ambrose, 1971, *La Pénitence* ['On Penance'], Roger Gryson (ed. and trans.), *Sources Chrétiennes* no. 179, Paris: Cerf.

Augustine of Hippo, 1950–1954, *City of God*, Demetrius B. Zema, Gerald G. Walsh, Grace Monahan and Daniel J. Honan (trans), 3 vols, New York: Fathers of the Church.

Augustine of Hippo, 1961, *Confessions*, R. S. Pine-Coffin (trans.), Harmondsworth: Penguin.

Augustine of Hippo, 1984, *The Rule of Saint Augustine: Masculine and Feminine Versions*, Raymond Channing (trans.), London: Darton, Longman & Todd.

Augustine of Hippo, 2016, *Questions on the Heptateuch*, Joseph T. Lienhard and Sean Doyle (trans), *The Writings of St. Augustine: A Translation for the 21st Century*, I/4, New York: New City Press of the Focolare.

Basil of Caesarea, 2001, *On the Holy Spirit*, David Anderson (trans.), Crestwood, NY: St Vladimir's Seminary Press.

Bede the Venerable, 1830, *Super Epistolas Catholicas Expositio* ['Exposition of the Catholic Epistles'], in Migne, J.-P. (ed.), *Venerabilis Bedae Anglosaxonis Presbyteri Opera Omnia*, *Patrologia Latina* 93, Paris, 1–130.

Clement of Alexandria, 1954, *Christ the Educator*, Simon P. Wood (trans.), New York: Fathers of the Church.

Cyril of Alexandria, 2019, *Commentary on the Second Letter to the Corinthians*, Konrad F. Zawadzki (ed.), *Der Kommentar Cyrills von*

Alexandrien zum 2. Korintherbrief: Einleitung, kritischer Text, Übersetzung, Einzelanalyse, Leiden: Brill.

Dante Alighieri, 1980, *The Divine Comedy*, C. H. Sisson (trans.), Oxford: Oxford University Press.

Dante Alighieri, 1992, *Vita Nova*, Mark Musa (trans.), Oxford: Oxford University Press.

Death of Pilate, the, 1924, in Montague Rhodes James (trans.), *The Apocryphal New Testament: Being the Apocryphal Gospels, Acts, Epistles, and Apocalypses, with Other Narratives and Fragments*, Oxford: Clarendon Press, pp. 157–79.

Doctrine of Addai, 1981, George Howard (trans.), Chico, CA: Scholars Press.

1 Enoch, *Ethiopic Apocalypse of Enoch*, E. Isaac OTP (ed. and trans.), pp. 5–89.

2 Enoch, *The Slavonic Apocalypse of Enoch*, Merilo Pravednoe and F. I. Andersen, OTP (eds and trans), pp. 91–221.

Eusebius, 1926, *Ecclesiastical History*, Kirsopp Lake (trans.), vol. 1, Loeb Classical Library, London: William Heinemann/New York: G. P. Putnam's Sons.

Evagrius Scholasticus, 2000, *Ecclesiastical History*, Michael Whitby (ed. and trans.), Liverpool: Liverpool University Press.

Give Me a Word: The Alphabetical Sayings of the Desert Fathers, 2015, John Wortley (trans.), London: SPCK.

Gregory the Great, 1959, *Dialogues*, Odo John Zimmerman (trans.), New York: Fathers of the Church, Inc.

Gregory of Nyssa, 1978, *Life of Moses*, Abraham J. Malherbe and Everett Ferguson (eds and trans), New York: Paulist Press; Greek text: Gregorio di Nissa, 1984, *La Vita di Mosè*, Manlio Simonetti (ed.), Verona: Arnoldo Mondadori.

Gregory Palamas (Gregory of Thessalonica), 1865, *On Divinity* [*De Divinitatis et rerum divinarum communicabilitate et incommunicabilitate*, 'On divinity and on the communicability and non-communicability of divine realities'], in Gregory Palamas, *Opera omnia ... quae supersunt*, J.-P. Migne (ed.), *Patrologiae Graeca*, vol. 150, Paris, columns 909–60.

Gregory Palamas (Gregory of Thessalonica), 1865, *Prosopopoeia* ['Speeches in character'], in Gregory Palamas, *Opera omnia ... quae supersunt*, J.-P. Migne (ed.), *Patrologiae Graeca* vol. 150, Paris, columns 1347–71.

Irenaeus, 2002, *Irenaeus's Demonstration of the Apostolic Preaching: A Theological Commentary and Translation*, Iain M. MacKenzie (ed.); with the translation of the text of the *Demonstration* by J. Armitage Robinson, Aldershot: Ashgate.

Jacob of Voragine, 2012, *The Golden Legend*, William Granger Ryan (trans.), new edition, Princeton, NJ: Princeton University Press.

John Chrysostom, 1889, *Saint Chrysostom: Homilies on the Gospel of St John and the Epistle to the Hebrews*, Oxford (trans.), P. Schaff (ed.), in *A Select Library of the Nicene and Post-Nicene Fathers of the Christian Church* vol. 14, Grand Rapids, MI: Wm. B. Eerdmans.

John Chrysostom, 1889, *On the Priesthood*, W. R. W. Stephens (trans.), in P. Schaff (ed.), *A Select Library of the Nicene and Post-Nicene Fathers of the Christian Church*, Grand Rapids, MI: Wm. B. Eerdmans.

John Damascene (John of Damascus), 2003, *Three Treatises on the Divine Images*, Andrew Louth (trans.), Crestwood, NY: St Vladimir's Seminary Press.

Justin Martyr, 1997, *The First and Second Apologies*, Leslie Barnard (ed. and trans.), Mahway, NJ: Paulist Press.

(Pseudo-) Macarius, 1860, *Homilies*, in *Macarii Aegyptii, Macarii Alexandrini, Opera quae supersunt omnia*, J.-P. Migne (ed.), *Patrologiae Graeca* vol. 34, Paris.

Merkavah Rabbah, see Schäfer 1982.

Nicholas of Cusa, 1997, *On the Vision of God*, in Nicholas of Cusa, *Selected Spiritual Writings*, H. Lawrence Bond (trans. and intro.), New York/Mahwah, NJ: Paulist Press, pp. 235–89.

Oecumenius, 1881, *Commentary on the Catholic Epistle of James* [*Jacobi Apostoli Epistola Catholica*], in Migne, J.-P. (ed.), *Oecumenii, Triccae in Thessalia Episcopi, Opera Omnia, Patrologia Graeca* 119, Paris, 455–510.

Philo, 1935, *Moses*, in *Philo* vol. 6, F. H. Colson (trans.), Loeb Classical Library, London: William Heinemann.

Plato, 1998, *Symposium*, C. J. Rowe (ed. and trans.), Warminster: Aris & Phillips Ltd.

Plato, 2013, *The Republic*, books 6–10, Chris Emlyn-Jones and William Preddy (trans), Loeb Classical Library, Cambridge, MA/London: Harvard University Press.

Plotinus, 1984, *Enneads*, A. H. Armstrong (trans.), Loeb Classical Library, Cambridge, MA: Harvard University Press/London: William Heinemann.

Possidius, 1954, *The Life of St. Augustine*, in F. R. Hoare (ed. and trans.), *The Western Fathers: being the lives of SS. Martin of Tours, Ambrose, Augustine of Hippo, Honoratus of Arles and Germanus of Auxerre*, London: Sheed & Ward, pp. 191–244.

Roman Missal, the, 2011, London: The Catholic Truth Society.

Shepherd of Hermas, the, 1999, Helmut Koester and Carolyn Osiek (eds and trans), Minneapolis, MN: Fortress Press.

Theodore the Studite, 2001, *On the Holy Icons*, Catharine P. Roth (trans.), Crestwood, NY: St Vladimir's Seminary Press.

Theophylact, 1864, *An Accurate Exposition of the Catholic Epistles*, in

Migne, J.-P. (ed.), *Theophylacti Bulgariae Archiepiscopi Opera Quae Reperiri Potuerunt Omnia, Patrologia Graeca* 125, Paris, 1131–1288.

Theophylact, 2007, *The Explanation of the Holy Gospel According to John*, Christopher Stade (trans.), House Springs, MO: Chrysostom Press.

Thérèse of Lisieux (Thérèse Martin), 1958, *Autobiography of a Saint*, Ronald Knox (trans.), London: Harvill Press.

Thomas Aquinas, 1997, *Catena Aurea: A Commentary on the four Gospels Collected out of the works of the Father by St Thomas Aquinas* (CA), J. H. Newman (ed.), 1841, republished Southampton: St Austin Press.

Thomas Aquinas, *c.* 1963, *Summa Theologiae*, Thomas Gilbey et al. (trans), London: Blackfriars with Eyre & Spottiswood.

Thomas Aquinas and Peter of Tarantaise, 2012, *Commentary on the Letters of Saint Paul to the Corinthians*, J. Mortensen and E. Alarcón (eds), F. R. Larcher et al. (trans), Lander, WY: The Aquinas Institute for the Study of Sacred Doctrine.

Collections

Charlesworth, James H. (ed.), 1983, *The Old Testament Pseudepigrapha*, vol. 1, London: Darton, Longman & Todd, pp. 5–89.

Jung, C. G., 1969, *Collected Works*, Gerhard Adler, Michael Fordham and Herbert Read (eds), R. F. C. Hull, Leopold Stein, Diana Riviere et al. (trans), 20 vols, 2nd edition, London: Routledge.

Secondary sources

Agliata, Daniel, and Stacey Tantleff-Dunn, 2004, 'The Impact of Media Exposure on Males' Body Image', *Journal of Social and Clinical Psychology* 23.1, pp. 7–22.

Albertson, David, 2019, 'Before the Icon: The Figural Matrix of *De Visione Dei*', in Thomas M. Izbicki, Jason Aleksander, and Donald F. Dunclow (eds), *Nicholas of Cusa and Times of Transition: Essays in Honor of Gerald Christianson*, Leiden: Brill, pp. 262–85.

Ammicht-Quinn, Regina, 2009, 'Cult, Culture and Ambivalence: Images and Imaginations of the Body in Christian Traditions and Contemporary Lifestyles', in Barbara Baert (ed.), *Fluid Flesh: The Body, Religion and the Visual Arts*, Leuven: Leuven University Press, pp. 67–81.

Barker, Margaret, 2003, *The Great High Priest: The Temple Roots of Christian Liturgy*, London: T & T Clark.

Barker, Margaret, 2010, *Creation: A Biblical Vision for the Environment*, London: T & T Clark.

Barker, Margaret, 2017, 'The Lead Books Found in Jordan', lecture to Temenos Academy, 2017, available online at www.leadbookcentre.com/publications.php (accessed 27 May 2019).

Barrett, C. K., 1973, *A Commentary on the Second Epistle to the Corinthians*, London: Adam & Charles Black.

Barrett, C. K., 1994, *A Critical and Exegetical Commentary on the Acts of the Apostles*, vol. 1, Edinburgh: T & T Clark.

Belting, Hans, 1994, *Likeness and Presence: A History of the Image Before the Era of Art*, Edmund Jephcott (trans.), Chicago, IL and London: University of Chicago Press.

Berset, R., 1976, *De commencement en commençant, Itinéraire d'une deviance*, Paris: Seuil.

Brown, David, 2007, *God and Grace of Body: Sacrament in Ordinary*, Oxford: Oxford University Press.

Caldecott, Stratford, 2013, *The Radiance of Being: Dimensions of Cosmic Christianity*, Tacoma, CO: Angelico Press.

Cameron, Avril, 1983, 'The History of the Image of Edessa: The Telling of a Story', *Harvard Ukrainian Studies*, pp. 80–94.

Carmody, Denise, 1995, *Christian Feminist Theology: A Constructive Interpretation*, Oxford: Blackwell.

Catechism of the Catholic Church, London: Geoffrey Chapman, 1994.

Clements, Ronald, 1972, *The Cambridge Bible Commentary on the New English Bible: Exodus*, Cambridge: Cambridge University Press.

Crawford, Kate, 2014, 'The Anxieties of Big Data', *The New Inquiry*, 30 May 2014, https://thenewinquiry.com/the-anxieties-of-big-data (accessed 29 October 2019).

Davis, Colin, 1996, *Levinas: An Introduction*, Cambridge: Polity Press, 1996.

de Certeau, Michel, 1987, 'The Gaze: Nicholas of Cusa', *Diacritics* 17, no. 3, pp. 2–38.

Deleuze, Gilles, and Félix Guattari, 1987, *A Thousand Plateaus: Capitalism and Schizophrenia*, Brian Massumi (trans.), Minneapolis, MN: University of Minnesota Press.

Dover, Kenneth, 1978, *Greek Homosexuality*, London: Duckworth.

Dozeman, Thomas B., 2009, *Commentary on Exodus*, Grand Rapids, MI: Wm. B. Eerdmans.

Dufresne, Mikel, 1973, *The Phenomenology of Aesthetic Experience*, Edward S. Casey et al. (trans), Evanston, IL: Northwestern University Press.

Eribon, Didier, 1991 [1989], *Michel Foucault*, Betsy Wing (trans.), Cambridge, MA: Harvard University Press.

Falcinelli, Roberto, 2010, 'The face of Manoppello and the Veil of

Veronica: New Studies', Proceedings of the International Workshop on the Scientific Approach to the Acheiropoietos Images, ENEA Frascati, Italy, 4–6 May 2010, www.acheiropoietos.info/proceedings/FalcinelliManoppelloWeb.pdf (accessed 29 November 2019).

Falque, Emmanuel, 2014, 'L'omnivoyant: Fraternité et vision de Dieu chez Nicolas de Cuse', *Revue des sciences philosophiques et théologiques* 98, no. 1, pp. 37–73. (Translation forthcoming in *Modern Theology*.)

Foucault, Michel, 1973 [1963], *The Birth of the Clinic: An Archaeology of Medical Perception*, A. M. Sheridan (trans.), London: Tavistock.

Foucault, Michel, 1977 [1975], *Discipline and Punish: The Birth of the Prison*, Alan Sheridan (trans.), Harmondsworth: Penguin.

Francis, Pope (Jorge Bergoglio), Post-Synodal Apostolic Exhortation *Amoris Laetitia* ('The Joy of Love'), London: Catholic Truth Society, 2016, available online at https://w2.vatican.va/content/dam/francesco/pdf/apost_exhortations/documents/papa-francesco_esortazione-ap_20160319_amoris-laetitia_en.pdf (accessed 28 June 2019).

Furnham, Adrian, 1996, 'Why Do People Choose and Use Complementary Therapies?', in Edzard Ernst (ed.), *Complementary Medicine: An Objective Appraisal*, Oxford: Butterworth-Heinemann, pp. 71–88.

Gamman, Lorraine, 1988, 'Watching the Detectives: the Enigma of the Female Gaze', in Lorraine Gamman and Margaret Marshment (eds), *The Female Gaze: Woman as Viewers of Popular Culture*, London: The Women's Press, pp. 8–26.

Gaucher, Guy, 1987, *The Story of a Life: St. Thérèse of Lisieux*, San Francisco, CA: HarperCollins.

Hadjadj, Fabrice, 2012, *Comment parler de Dieu aujourd'hui? Anti-manuel d'évangélisation* ['How to speak about God today? An anti-manual of evangelisation'], Paris: Salvator.

Handelman, Susan, 1990, 'Facing the Other: Levinas, Perelman and Rosenzweig, Religion & Literature', vol. 22, no. 2/3, *Religious Thought and Contemporary Critical Theory*, pp. 61–84.

Henderson, David, 2010, 'The Coincidence of Opposites: C. G. Jung's Reception of Nicholas of Cusa', *Studies in Spirituality* 20, pp. 101–13.

Hoff, Johannes, 2013, 'The Visibility of the Invisible: From Nicholas of Cusa to Late Modernity and Beyond', in Louise Nelstrop and Simon Podmore (eds), *Christian Mysticism and Incarnational Theology: Between Transcendence and Immanence*, Burlington, VT: Ashgate, pp. 47–68.

Horner, Robyn, 2005, *Jean-Luc Marion: A* Theo-*Logical Introduction*, Aldershot: Ashgate.

Houtman, Cornelis, 2000, *Exodus*, vol. 3 (chs 20–40), Sierd Woustra (trans.), Leuven: Peeters.

Hunt, Elle, 2019, 'Later-in-life Virgins – "At My Age, it Becomes a Red Flag"', *The Guardian*, 18 June 2019, available online at www.theguardian.com/lifeandstyle/2019/jun/18/later-in-life-virgins-at-my-age-it-becomes-a-red-flag (accessed 1 July 2019).

Information Commissioner's Office, 2018, *Guide to the General Data Protection Regulation (GDPR)*, https://ico.org.uk/for-organisations/guide-to-data-protection/guide-to-the-general-data-protection-regulation-gdpr (accessed 5 December 2019).

Jay, Martin, 1993, *The Denigration of Vision in Twentieth-Century French Thought*, Berkeley, CA/Los Angeles/London: University of California Press.

Jensen, Robin M., 2011, *Living Water: Images, Symbols, and Settings of Early Christian Baptism*, Leiden/Boston, MA: Brill.

Johnson, Luke Timothy, 1995, *The Letter of James: A New Translation with Introduction and Commentary*, New Haven, CT, and London: Yale University Press.

Jones, Alexandra, 2018, 'I Tried "Instagram Face" for a Week and Here's what Happened ... The Rise of Selfie Make-up and Our Quest for Hyper-perfection', BBC website, 17 August 2018, www.bbc.co.uk/bbcthree/article/5c237a34-7a47-4deb-a5b4-a23e77cc88f7 (accessed 16 December 2019).

Jung, Carl, 1969, 'Basic Postulates of Analytical Psychology' (1), Jung CW vol. 8, pp. 649–88.

Jung, Carl, 1970, 'A Psychological Approach to the Dogma of the Trinity', Jung CW vol. 11, pp. 168–243.

Jurgenson, Nathan, 2019, *The Social Photo: On Photography and Social Media*, London/Brooklyn, NY: Verso.

Kaplan, E. Ann, 1979, 'Avant-garde Feminist Cinema: Mulvey and Wollen's *Riddles of the Sphinx*', *Quarterly Review of Film Studies*, 1979, issue 2, pp. 135–48.

Kelly, J. N. D., 1969, *A Commentary on the Epistles of Peter and of Jude*, London: A & C Black.

Kelly, Yvonne, Afshin Zilanawala, Cara Booker, and Amanda Sacker, 2019, 'Social Media Use and Adolescent Mental Health: Findings from the UK Millennium Cohort Study', *EClinicalMedicine*, January 2019 (open access at www.sciencedirect.com/science/article/pii/S2589537018300609?via%3Dihub, accessed 9 January 2019). The study, which at the time of writing is ongoing, is based on population data from the UK Millennium Cohort Study of 10,904 14-year-olds.

Lacan, Jacques, 1968, 'The Mirror-phase as Formative of the Function of the I', *New Left Review* 51, pp. 71–7.

Lacan, Jacques, 1978, *Seminar XI: The Four Fundamental Concepts of Psychoanalysis*, Jacques Alain Miller (ed.), Alan Sheridan (trans.), New York and London: W.W. Norton and Co.

Lacan, Jacques, 1988, *Seminar One: Freud's Papers On Technique 1953–1954*, John Forrester (trans.), Cambridge: Cambridge University Press.

Lamm, Kimberly, 2018, *Addressing the Other Woman: Textual Correspondences in Feminist Art and Writing*, Manchester: Manchester University Press.

Lemeni, Daniel, 2016, '"Shining Face and White Body": Holy Flesh and Holiness in the Spirituality of the Desert', *International Journal of Orthodox Theology* 7.4, pp. 38–53.

Levinas, Emmanuel, 1969 [1961], *Totality and Infinity: An Essay on Exteriority*, Alphonso Lingis (trans.), Pittsburgh, PA: Duquesne University Press.

Levinas, Emmanuel, 1978, *Existence and Existents*, Alphonso Lingis (trans.), The Hague: M. Nijhoff.

Levinas, Emmanuel, 1981 [1974], *Otherwise than Being: Or Beyond Essence*, Alphonso Lingis (trans.), Pittsburgh, PA: Duquesne University Press.

Lion, Antoine, 2005, '"Nous l'avons fait." Fondements d'un combat spirituel' ['"We've done it." The foundations of a spiritual battle'], *Mémoires Dominicaines*, vol. 6, pp. 43–56.

Lossky, Vladimir, 1976, *The Mystical Theology of the Eastern Church*, Crestwood, NY: St Vladimir's Seminary Press.

Lottman, Herbert R., 1979, *Albert Camus: A Biography*, London: Weidenfeld & Nicolson.

Marion, Jean-Luc, 1995, *God Without Being*, Thomas A. Carlson (trans.), Chicago, IL/London: University of Chicago Press.

Marion, Jean-Luc, 2002, *Prolegomena to Charity*, Stephen Lewis (trans.), New York: Fordham University Press.

Marion, Jean-Luc, 2016, 'Seeing, or Seeing Oneself Seen: Nicholas of Cusa's Contribution in *De Visione Dei*', *The Journal of Religion* 96, no. 3 (July 2016), pp. 305–31.

Maté, Gabor, 2019, *When the Body Says No: The Cost of Hidden Stress*, new edn, London: Vermilion.

McAuley, Joseph, 'When a Pope Met a First Lady: "Ah, Jacqueline!"', *America: The Jesuit Review*, 18 September 2015, www.americamagazine.org/content/all-things/when-pope-made-fuss-over-first-lady-john-xxiii-and-mrs-kennedy-ah-jacqueline (accessed 16 January 2020).

McCabe, Herbert, 1987, 'The Involvement of God', in Herbert McCabe, *God Matters*, London and New York: Mowbray, pp. 39–51.

McCosker, Anthony, 2015, 'Drone Media: Unruly Systems, Radical Empiricism and Camera Consciousness', *Culture Machine*, vol. 16, https://culturemachine.net/drone-culture/drone-media/ (accessed 29 October 2019).

Mcfarland, Ian, 2016, 'What Does It Mean To See Someone? Icons and Identity', in Jeffrey Barbeau and Beth Felker Jones (eds), *The Image of God in an Image-Driven Age: Explorations in Theological Anthropology*, Downers Grove, IL: InterVarsity Press, pp. 157–72.

McHugh, John F., 2009, *John 1–4: A Critical and Exegetical Commentary*, London: T & T Clark.

Meagher, P. K., 1967, 'VERONICA', in *New Catholic Encyclopedia*, New York: McGraw-Hill, vol. 14, p. 625.

Merleau-Ponty, Maurice, 1960, *The Visible and the Invisible*, Alphonso Lingis (trans.), Evanston, IL: Northwestern University Press.

Meyers, Carol, 2005, *Exodus*, Cambridge: Cambridge University Press.

Mills, Jennifer S., Sarah Musto, Lindsay Williams, Marika Tiggemann, 2018, '"Selfie" Harm: Effects on Mood and Body Image in Young Women', *Body Image* 27, pp. 86–92.

Mounier, Emmanuel, 1947, *Introduction aux Existentialismes* ['Introduction to Existentialisms'], in Œuvres, vol. 3, Paris, Seuil, 1962, pp. 67–175.

Mulvey, Laura, 1975, 'Visual Pleasure and Narrative Cinema', in Leo Braudy and Marshall Cohen (eds), 1999, *Film Theory and Criticism: Introductory Readings*, New York: Oxford University Press, pp. 833–44 (originally published in *Screen*, 16/3, pp. 6–18).

NHS England, 2018, 'Shared Decision Making: About', www.england.nhs.uk/shared-decision-making/about/ (accessed 22 November 2018).

Nichols, Aidan, 1980, *The Art of God Incarnate: Theology and Image in Christian Tradition*, London: Darton, Longman & Todd.

O'Mahony, Christopher (ed. and trans.), 1975, *St Thérèse of Lisieux by Those Who Knew Her: Testimonies from the Process of Beatification*, Dublin: Veritas.

Ouspensky, Leonid, and Vladimir Lossky, 1982, *The Meaning of Icons*, G. E. H. Palmer and E. Kadloubovsky (trans), New York: St Vladimir's Seminary Press.

Ouspensky, Leonid, 1992, *Theology of the Icon*, 2 vols, Anthony Gythiel and Elizabeth Meyendorff (trans), Crestwood, NY: St Vladimir's Seminary Press.

Pfeiffer, Heinrich, 1986, *L'Immagine di Cristo nell'Arte* ['The Image of Christ in Art'], Rome: Città Nuova.

Pfeiffer, Heinrich, 2000, *Il Volto Santo di Manoppello* ['The Holy Face of Manoppello'], Pescara: CARSA.

Pickstock, Catherine, 1998, *After Writing: On the Liturgical Consummation of Philosophy*, Oxford/Malden, MA: Blackwell.

Potok, Chaim, 1990, *The Gift of Asher Lev*, London: Heinemann.

Radcliffe, Timothy, 2019, *Alive in God: A Christian Imagination*, London: Bloomsbury.

Ranke-Heinemann, Uta, 1990, *Eunuchs for the Kingdom of God: The Catholic Church and Sexuality*, John Brownjohn (trans.), London: André Deutsch.

Rist, Anna, 2005, *We Etruscans: Old and New in a Forgotten Landscape*, Cambridge: Lutterworth Press.

Ryindina, A. V., 2001, 'Anchiyskiy Spas' ['The Saviour of Ancha'], in *Orthodox Encyclopaedia*, vol. 3, pp. 16–17, available online at www.pravenc.ru/text/75560.html (accessed 25 November 2019).

Rogers, Ann (ed.), *c.* 2001, 'Background paper on the Expert Patients' Programme for NICE Expert Testimony', Expert Paper 1, www.nice.org.uk/guidance/ph19/evidence/expert-paper-1-pdf-371292301 (accessed 22 November 2018).

Roncalli, Angelo (St John XXIII), 1980, *Journal of a Soul*, D. White (trans.), London: Geoffrey Chapman.

Rosenzweig, Franz, 2005 [1920], *The Star of Redemption*, Barbara E. Galli (trans.), Madison, WI: University of Wisconsin Press.

Salk, Rachel H., and Renee Engeln-Maddox, 2011, '"If You're Fat, Then I'm Humongous!": Frequency, Content, and Impact of Fat Talk Among College Women', *Psychology of Women Quarterly*, 35 (1), pp. 18–28.

Sartre, Jean-Paul, 1956, 'The Look', in Jean-Paul Sartre, *Being and Nothingness, An Essay on Phenomenological Ontology*, Hazel E. Barnes (trans.), New York: Philosophical Library, pp. 253–6.

Sassatelli, Roberta, 2011, 'Interview with Laura Mulvey: Gender, Gaze and Technology in Film Culture', *Theory, Culture & Society*, vol. 28/5, pp. 123–43.

Schaefer, Jean Owens, 1986, 'St. Luke as Painter; From Saint to Artisan to Artist', in X. Barral i Altet (ed.), *Artistes, artisans et production artistique au Moyen Âge*, Paris: Flammarion, vol. 1, p. 413–27.

Schäfer, P., 1982, *The Hidden and Manifest God*, New York: State University of New York Press.

Shaw, Joanna, 2004, '"Expert Patient" – Dream or Nightmare?', *British Medical Journal,* 328; www.bmj.com/content/328/7442/723 (accessed 5 November 2019).

Sherrard, Philip, 1962, 'The Art of the Icon', *Sobornost* IV.6, pp. 294–303.

Shortt, Rupert, 2019, 'Mad Virgins and Don Juans', *Times Literary Supplement*, 19 April 2019.

Sigurdson, Ola, 2016, *Heavenly Bodies: Incarnation: The Gaze, and Embodiment in Christian Theology*, Carl Olsen (trans.), Grand Rapids, MI: Wm. B. Eerdmans.

Singh, Simon, and Edzard Ernst, 2008, *Trick or Treatment? Alternative Medicine on Trial*, London: Bantam.

Sontag, Susan, 1978 [1977], *On Photography*, London: Penguin.

Stallabrass, Julian, 1996, *Gargantua: Manufactured Mass Culture*, London: Verso Books.

Steele, Valerie, 2001, *The Corset: A Cultural History*, New Haven, CT and London: Yale University Press, 2001, pp. 70–1.

Tiggemann, Marika, and Brenda McGill, 2004, 'The Role of Social Comparison in the Effect of Magazine Advertisements on Women's Mood and Body Dissatisfaction', *Journal of Social and Clinical Psychology*, 23.1, pp. 23–44.

Uitvlugt, Donald Jacob, 1998, '"Ta Face est ma seule Patrie" (PN 20): The Holy Face in the Spirituality of St. Therese of Lisieux', *Catholic Dossier*, October 1998, https://web.archive.org/web/19991111202014/http://catholic.net/RCC/Periodicals/Dossier/MARAPR99/seule.html (accessed 26 November 2019).

Varden, Erik, 2018, *The Shattering of Loneliness: On Christian Remembrance*, London: Bloomsbury Continuum.

Vettori, Alessandro, 2003, 'Veronica: Dante's Pilgrimage from Image to Vision', *Dante Studies, with the Annual Report of the Dante Society*, no. 121, pp. 43–65.

White, Dominic, 2015, *The Lost Knowledge of Christ: Contemporary Spiritualities, Christian Cosmology, and the Arts*, Collegeville, MN: The Liturgical Press.

White, Dominic, 2017, *How Do I Look? Bodies and the Theotic Gaze*, The Holy Biscuit Blog, www.theholybiscuit.org/how-do-i-look-bodies-and-the-theotic-gaze/ (accessed 14 January 2020).

White, Dominic, 2019, 'Why the Body Needs Plato (and Plato Needs the Body)', Margaret Beaufort Institute of Theology blog post, www.margaretbeaufort.cam.ac.uk/2019/04/09/why-the-body-needs-plato-and-plato-needs-the-body/ (accessed 1 July 2019).

Williams, Rowan, 1996, 'The Body's Grace', in Charles Hefling (ed.), *Our Selves, Our Souls and Bodies: Sexuality and the House of God*, Cambridge/Boston, MA: Cowley Publications, pp. 58–68.

Williams, Rowan, 2000, *Lost Icons: Reflections on Cultural Bereavement*, Edinburgh: T & T Clark.

Wojtyła, Karol (St John Paul II), 1981 [1960], *Love and Responsibility*, H. T. Willets (trans.), San Francisco, CA: Ignatius.

Yegül, Fikret, 2010, *Bathing in the Roman World*, Cambridge: Cambridge University Press.

Index of Names and Subjects